A Taste of Ranching

Cooks & Cowboys

A Taste of Ranching

Cooks & Cowboys

by
Tom Bryant and Joel Bernstein

Border Books

Albuquerque, New Mexico

Edited by Jim Burbank
Melissa T. Stock, Editorial Director
Book Design by Lois Bergthold

Printed in the United States of America

ISBN 0-9623865-7-X

Cowboy Gettin'-up Hollers

Wake up, Jacob, day's a-breakin';
Fryin' pan's on an' hoecake bakin'.
Bacon in the pan, coffee in the pot;
Get up now and get it while it's hot.

❧

Wake up, snakes, and bite a biscuit.

❧

Rise and shine, and give God the glory.

❧

Roll out there, fellers, and hear the little birdies
sing their praises to God.

❧

Grub pile! Come a-runnin', boys!

❧

Hungry enough to eat a saddle blanket.

Cowboy Graces

Eat your meat and save the skin;
Turn up your plates and let's begin.

❧

Thar's the bread, thar's the meat;
Now, by Joe, let's eat.

CONTENTS

Foreword

Ranching has been a part of the western heritage for more than a century. The challenges have always been difficult—and that hasn't changed much. In addition to the ever-present challenges of hard winters, blistering summer days and uncertain cattle prices, a whole new set of challenges face today's ranchers, cowboys and others making their living on ranches. False claims about land use, attacks on their way of life, their product and their property are everyday facts of life for folks out West.

But this country's original environmentalists and land stewards just turn up their collars, tell the truth to those who will listen and keep doing what they do best—taking care of the land and the cattle and providing people around the world with a high-quality source of protein raised on renewable resources.

They don't do it because this is an easy way of life. They do it because they love the wide open spaces, the people around them and a way of life that is quickly disappearing in today's hustling, bustling, ever-shrinking world.

Ranching has a way of grabbing the imagination. There's something about sitting on a horse and looking over a green meadow dotted with cows and calves that pulls at the heart strings and keeps ranchers out in the blistering heat and the frigid cold tending stock, tending dreams, tending an American tradition.

A Taste of Ranching takes you to places where that tradition is still alive, where snow-capped peaks touch cool, blue skies and rushing rivers wind icy fingers toward the sparkling mountain meadows of the West.

Today, as they have for generations, the people who live here share their stories, spin their yarns and open up their hearts and kitchens to the traveler in need of a hot meal. Their lives and their recipes are flavored with the spices, warmth and humor of the West. The National Cattlemen's Association represents many of these ranchers and cowboys who call the West their home.

Today, the business of ranching is alive and well, and *A Taste of Ranching* brings you a taste of North America's ranching lifestyle in all its flavor and warmth. Like the National Cattlemen's Association, *A Taste of Ranching* is doing its share to preserve the breath-taking vistas, heart-warming recipes and ever-expansive souls of the West.

I invite you to explore *A Taste of Ranching* and taste the North American West.

Sincerely,
Jimme Wilson, Past President
National Cattlemen's Association

INTRODUCTION

Part I
by Tom Bryant

The image of the ranch cook is as old as the West itself. We all have pictures in our mind of the grizzled old cook who ruled his domain with an iron pan and a voice that would peel paint off the walls or scorch the grass in a 20-foot circle.

No cowboy, cowboss, owner or visitor crossed the cook. Good cooks were hard to find, and still are. It used to be common practice for ranches to try to lure a good cook from a neighboring ranch by bribery, begging, or sometimes just plain shanghaiing. Ranches that had a good cook usually were real careful to keep it a secret.

A top-notch cook could keep cowboys working in spite of bad weather, low pay, loco cows, mean horses, impersonal bosses and absentee owners. A good ranch cook was, and is, the epicenter of a smooth working cow outfit.

After leaving a well-paying city job in 1981, I started doing some free-lance writing to supplement cowboying wages in Montana. It was in the Stoudier cowcamp of the Matador Cattle Company in the Centennial Valley south of Dillon that I began to realize the power and importance of a ranch cook.

Bill Humphrey was the cook, and he woke the cowboys up at 3:30 a.m. screaming, "You're burning daylight!" I thought old Bill had seen too many movies, because daylight was a long way off. Bill filled the boys up on sourdough pancakes and lick (syrup), sausage, eggs and hot coffee.

As they finished eating, the cowboys dumped their eating utensils in the sink and each said, "Thank you Bill," as they filed out the door. Bill brightened for the first time that day. "Come back at lunch time and we'll do 'er again," he said.

I was on a story assignment, and after the riders left I got to visiting with Bill. I found a very interesting individual, one who had seen a lot of living, and who could work and talk at the same time. He snubbed out a smoke and started rolling out dough. "Making pies for the boys," he said. "Cowboys are big on desserts, don't you know?"

That was a comment I was to hear many times as I visited some 40 ranches during the next two years. I finished my coffee and visited with Bill until the sun came up and I left to start shooting photographs of the fall roundup.

I never saw Bill Humphrey again. Like many old-time cowboys and cooks, he was a rambler. He talked about going to California to look for gold, or maybe to Alaska. Fantasies to follow. Dreams to pass the time while you knead dough or wash dishes or muck out the kitchen. As the sun came up over the mountains, I shook hands with Bill and wished him well.

He gave me a dream and a goal that has been the driving force in my life ever since. I realized that on many ranches, the cook is usually the most underrated hand in the outfit, and singularly the most important. They may see life out the window of a kitchen, but it is real life they see, and most all have a tale or two to tell. On most ranches, the kitchen and dining area serve as a meeting room, the center of the storm of activities that occurs within an outfit every day.

The ranch work day begins in the kitchen. It is here that the boss takes head count and sorts out who is to do what that day. Assignments are given out over coffee. If the hands return at noon, lunch becomes a midday staff meeting where progress and problems are discussed, decisions handed down and reassignments made.

Dinner or supper on a ranch is not usually served until the work is all done for the day. At that time, a recap of the day's activities is made and plans are made for tomorrow. The kitchen is the command post, the mess center, the gossip center, the gathering and story-telling center. The kitchen is the heart of a ranch, and the cook is the soul of the outfit. The kitchen provides the energy for the outfit, but it is the cook that makes it work.

I discussed ranching and cooking with my friend and riding partner, Joel Bernstein, and we set out to gather information for a book on cowboys and cooks. Joel took out a second mortgage on his small ranch and we hit the road. We have driven over much of the West interviewing cowboys, ranchers and cooks. It has been both educational and entertaining.

I flew to Sacramento, where my brother-in-law, Jim Adams, let me have a '78 Dodge van, and I was off on my odyssey. I rode with ranchers in rainstorms, thunderstorms, lightning storms, and blizzards. I sat in kitchens and watched the cooks make magic. Watched cowboys and ranch hands relive work and wrecks and dream out loud about girls and town, pickups, bucking horses and bad bovines.

The book project has been a lot of fun, but also extremely difficult for me. I'm slightly dyslexic, and am the world's worst typist, and cannot even spell my name correctly on most days. If not for my ex-wife Nancy's constant supervision, this book would never have been completed.

To my sisters Ruth Briezy, Dot Adams, Nelle Wells and their husbands, to my brothers Gene, James, Ken and Joe, I'll be forever thankful for your support and belief in me. By just being there, you have helped me more than you'll ever know.

And to my partner Joel I am especially grateful for not only riding with me, but for becoming a part of the project and a driving force in the long and painful process of finding a publisher. And I want to thank our publisher, Robert Spiegel, and his lovely wife Jill for believing in Joel and me and backing this book. Read it and enjoy it; try the recipes and get a real Taste of Ranching.

Part II
by Joel H. Bernstein

Like so many Americans, I too, as a boy growing up, was fascinated by the West—and mostly by the cowboys. I don't know exactly why—maybe it was the influence of the Saturday morning serials at the movies or even the radio—but whatever it was, the romance never left me.

When I was in the fourth grade, I told my father that I wanted to be a cowboy. And because my parents at least took me at my word (not bad for a fourth-grader), my life has been different, and at times exciting and interesting beyond my own dreams. My dad and I took riding lessons for two years. Those years were to set a foundation that would last me the rest of my life. Many years later, in the early 1960s, when I had my first riding job and I started rodeoing in Wyoming, those riding lessons sure were a comfort.

Over the years, whether running my own outfit in Montana, or cowboying for outfits in Wyoming and Montana, the puncher's life changed only in detail, never in attitude. It's not a job you take for the money—heck, my first job paid the princely sum of $30.00 per week plus room and board—but it's a way of life you choose. Over the years I've hardly met a cowboy who'd live his life differently. It makes little difference if you're the foreman, cowboss, cowpoke, wrangler or cook—you live a life that's rooted in the past, in the best traditions of North America. And yet, it's a life that is also present in the modern world, as cooks and cowboys search for their place in it, as we all do.

When Tom and I decided to do this book, we also decided to travel separately, because together we'd have too much fun and do too little work. We were also afraid that together we might just sign on some good working outfit even farther in the wilds than where we were living in Montana.

As I traveled, whether up in Alberta or down to the vast high desert country of southwestern New Mexico, the one thing that stands out is the friendliness and open acceptance I received from ranchers, cowboys, cooks and people whom oftentimes I had never even met before. They fed me, gave me a place to sleep, sometimes a day's work on horseback, and what I will always remember, they shared their lives with me—even for a brief time.

Lonnie and Mary Moore of the Gray Ranch took me to a monthly community dance in the small ranching community of Animas, New Mexico,where I met some of the most friendly and interesting people I'd met in a long time. Twylla Tyson introduced me to her neighbors and friends in western Alberta. And Shirley Bugli, an old friend from the Bitterroot Valley since the days when I was headin' up the rodeo team at the University of Montana, where her two daughters were star team members, shared her memories of days that, unfortunately, seem to be slipping away.

But all the cooks, whether they were wives of foremen, wives of cowboys, or solely cooks, had a wonderful sense of the values of the wide open spaces in an increasingly smaller world, and the independence and self-reliance associated with the cowboys on the range and frontier.

Tom and I owe these people our thanks, and they have certainly won our respect. It never fails to amaze me to see how fast you can become friends over a cup of coffee in a warm kitchen, leaning against some corral rails in the afternoon sun, or spending a couple of hours in the saddle riding over the range that has been home to buffalo and cattle for centuries. It sounds like a cliché to speak about ranching and ranch people this way, but it's true. People still live like this, and are proud of their lives and what they mean. Maybe that's why dude ranching continues to expand—city folks get a taste of this life, albeit a brief taste.

We've worked on this book for some years now, and since we got started, I moved to New Mexico. Tom and I still share an occasional visit, and we write and phone each other more often than either of us ever figured we'd do. But fortunately, I am spurred along by my best friend and love, Julie King, who never lets me get too lazy. When I want to be out training and riding horses, she wants to know why I'm not writing. And my family, my mother Addie and my sister and brother-in-law, Judi and Irvin Pressman, always took me seriously when I moved west more than 30 years ago to pursue my dreams. I thank you all. My father, who passed away some years ago, was in spirit a real cowboy, and I think of him often; of his guidance and support as I grew up and learned to search for the things that became important in my life.

And like Tom, I want to thank Robert Spiegel and his wife Jill for letting us write our book, and publishing it. Your help and support have meant a great deal to us. We've tried to let the ranch people tell their own stories with as little intrusion from us as possible. We hope we've succeeded, and more importantly, we hope we've given the reader a taste of ranching, with its cooks and cowboys. We'd just like to let you know that ranching, in the West is alive and well.

Finally to my partner Tom—you're a good man to ride the rivers with.

Feeding yearlings in winter in the Big Hole Valley of Montana.

SECTION I:
THE NORTHERN ROCKIES

...there is much work and hardship, rough fare, monotony and
exposure connected with the roundup, yet there are few men
who do not look forward to it and back to it with pleasure...

Theodore Roosevelt,
Ranch Life and the Hunting Trail,
Bonanza Books 1978

When we headed north across the border to Alberta, Canada, we anticipated little change from the U.S. in either the people or country. Over the years, we've been up to see our Canadian neighbors many times, and since we needed neither passport nor visa to cross the border at one of several entry ports between Alberta and Montana, we knew the border patrol would just ask a few friendly questions and then we would be on our way.

Visually at least, Alberta forms an extension of Montana. Or as Canadians like to say, Montana is just the lower part of Alberta. The province is comprised of 661,185 square kilometers, with sparse population, except in the cities of Calgary and Edmonton. An open land rich in natural resources, particularly oil and timber, Alberta features a varied and impressive landscape, stretching from rolling hills in the east, to glacial lakes, snow-capped mountains and the raw wilderness of the Canadian Rockies in the west, location of popular tourist areas such as Banff and Lake Louise.

Sometimes the names may differ between the two countries, but a ranch is still a ranch, no matter what. Texas has its Rangers and Canada has its Mounties, but traditions in the U.S. and our neighbor north of the border interlink, so without an international boundary line between our two countries, the visitor might be hard-pressed to know he or she was in a different country.

Alberta is every bit as much cowboy country as Montana, Wyoming or Colorado, and these lands still retain a quality all their own. Clean and spacious, the land spreads beneath a clear sky, with small towns dotting the landscape, preserving their own colorful frontier past.

In the mid-eighteenth century, fur traders and missionaries began to encroach on the Cree, Blackfoot (in the United States this tribe is called Blackfeet), Assiniboine, Sarcee and other tribes who were the original inhabitants of this magic land.

With the formation of Canada in 1867, Montana Territory whiskey traders began moving north along what was called the Whoop Up Trail to Fort Whoop Up, a notorious trading post where they sold illegal booze to the Indians.

In 1847, 300 members of the newly-formed Northwest Mounted Police left Dufferin, Manitoba on a 1,126-mile trek, to establish law and order on the western Canadian frontier--a prodigious undertaking, because of the vast expanses they had to patrol. When the Mounties arrived in what is now Alberta, they set up the first post, Fort Macleod, named for Colonel James F. Macleod, their commander, who carefully prepared their mission to bring law and order to this wild country. They quickly succeeded in taming the province, dramatically reducing the whiskey trade in just one short year, earning the respect of settlers and Indians alike. The detachment at Fort Macleod helped build an international reputation for the Mounties as a premier police force.

In 1882, Alberta became a province after being named for Princess Louise Alberta, daughter of Queen Victoria. Boundaries for the province were finally settled in 1905.

Blessed by plentiful water and fertile, black soil, central and eastern Alberta provide one of the richest agricultural areas of Canada. The province's tall-grass prairie country has made ranching and farming very productive. Canadian cowboy traditions and gear parallel those of their southern counterparts, and today bear a close resemblance to that of their contemporaries in Montana and Wyoming.

Few cowboy or rodeo fans in North America haven't heard of the Calgary Stampede, one of the truly great rodeos, held each July. The only Canadian sport to rival the popularity of rodeo in the province is ice hockey. Rodeo records reveal that some top bronc riders are Canadians. Cowboys such as Marty Wood, Winston Bruce, Malcolm Jones, Ivan Daines, Steve Dunham, Robin Burwash and many more come out of Alberta, where top hands have to handle some tough horses. Canada has also produced Reg Kesler, one of the greatest competitors, stock contractors and leaders in the Canadian and United States rodeo world.

Ranchers in Canada and the United States also share many of the same problems—drought, severe weather (particularly in winter), price fluctuations in the cattle market, rising costs, encroachments of towns on ranch lands and development of former ranch lands for non-agricultural uses. Though these difficulties persist, ranches still manage to survive, and Alberta ranching continues to be an important industry.

When we visited Canada, ranchers north of the border greeted us warmly, and in ranch kitchens poured us cups of steaming, black coffee, particularly on blustery winter days.

The conversations were easy; it struck us how quickly we were reminded that cowboys and ranchers have a certain way of sharing common experience, even if we had never met before.

We all know what it's like to assist a cow with her calf on a freezing winter day, or the warm and generous feel of being bone-weary from a day in the saddle and returning home to a glowing fire and a fine meal. And then there are those final minutes before your head hits the pillow at night, when you reflect on all that has gone on during that day, and you just can't wait to get up and do it all again the next day. Such commonality, such shared feelings build a warmth and comradeship based on the living tradition of ranching that has made the West the open and friendly place it remains today.

Edward, Prince of Wales at the EP Ranch with George Lane of the Bar U Ranch in Pekisko, Alberta, circa 1923. Courtesy of Glenbow Archives, Calgary, Alberta.

4

E P RANCH
PEKISKO, ALBERTA, CANADA

RANCH OF PRINCES
Lynn Cartwright, Royal Ranch Cook

Nestled among the pines and cottonwoods of Pekisko Creek in the eastern foothills of the Canadian Rockies, south of Calgary, the EP Ranch probably ranks as one of the most interesting and historically significant cattle ranches in North America.

In western Alberta during 1884, Frank Bedingfeld and his mother came from England to the High River country to homestead. Two years later they formed a partnership with a man known as George "7U" Brown, and together they bought a place on Pekisko Creek. The partnership lasted until 1919, when Brown got his own outfit.

In 1919, Edward, Prince of Wales, made his first Canadian visit to renew acquaintances, as he had promised, with former soldiers he had met in France during World War I. As was the fashion then, many young, wealthy Englishmen wanted to participate in the glamor and adventure of western North American ranching. Often they took part in these ventures as absentee owners.

Overwhelmed by his warm Canadian reception, Prince Edward, with the help of George Brown of the Bar U Ranch, headed west and saw what is now the EP Ranch. On the way back to the east coast following his visit, the Crown Prince decided to purchase the old Bedingfeld place. While he was still in Winnipeg, news of the sale reached England, where the King and Queen expressed fury that the future monarch had just bought a 4,000-acre ranch in provincial Canada.

A YOUNG PRINCE PREVAILS

But the young prince prevailed, renamed the place EP for Edward Prince, and established the EP brand used on both horses and cattle. The Prince had a real interest in agriculture and ranching when he bought the EP, and he planned to import quality livestock to help improve Canadian breeding. During the 43 years he owned the ranch, the Prince raised cattle, horses and a few hogs and sheep.

Though he seemed to like the Canadian ranch, royal duties seldom let him visit and involve himself in the operation, as he had once hoped.

In the 1920s, however, the Prince visited three times during American tours when he could take quick trips to the ranch for a week or two, mostly in spring or fall. On one trip in 1923, he traveled incognito as Lord Renfrew, the same alias used by the current Prince Charles when he dated the future Princess Diana.

Edward liked the cowboys, and the ranch gate was always open for them to visit. Local news media discovered his penchant for cowpokes, and reporters disguised as cowhands tried to enter the ranch for interviews until watchful Mounties discovered their deception and threw them out.

When at the ranch, the Prince tried to work with the crew as often as possible. His accessibility to the cowboys made him popular.

Nearby Turner Valley had proven out as the first major Alberta oil strike in 1914. Expecting oil and the potential for large profits on the EP property, the Prince decided to drill, but two holes came up dry, surprising him. Today, while the surrounding ranch country is marked by pumping wells, none are on the EP.

In January 1936 the Prince became King of England, but his reign lasted only a year when he abdicated to "marry the woman I love." The couple became Duke and Duchess of Windsor. The Duchess was none too crazy about the ranch in the Alberta wilds, preferring more elegant accommodations in Calgary. She seldom even wanted to see the ranch.

A DEAL IS STRUCK

In 1950, during their final visit to the EP, the Duchess finally convinced the Duke to sell the ranch. In February 1962, Jim Cartwright, whose family had homesteaded in the area before the turn of the century, purchased the EP. A warm Alberta chinook had raised temperatures 30-40 degrees in a matter of hours, melted snow and played havoc with roads and bridges, making it difficult for other prospective buyers even to see the ranch. But the Cartwrights were in the right place at the right time and struck a deal, buying the ranch for about $185,000.

Because of the Duke's infrequent visits and due to the fact he had in the last years of his ownership leased the EP to a consortium, the ranch had deteriorated. Fences and buildings needed repair, the land had been overrun by willows and several of the stately set of barns had burned.

But the Cartwrights needed the ranch to add to their winter range. They had ranched just west of the EP since 1909, so joining the new property with the D Ranch, which they already owned, seemed like a good move.

Now they produce about 600 calves yearly on the combined 48,000 acres of deeded and leased lands that make up their current spread. Jim Cartwright died in 1976 and now his two sons, John and Gordon, own the ranch. John runs the EP division and Gordon bosses the D Ranch.

When the Prince owned the property, he had allowed curious members of the public to visit, and when Jim bought the property, he continued this policy. In fact, on the deeded acreage, the Cartwrights have six campgrounds, so the public can stay overnight or picnic there on a free first-come-first-serve basis. The curious can even bring their own horses to ride, if they inform the Cartwrights in advance, and the family has even kept the ranch open for hunting in the foothill country.

John and Lynn Cartwright decided to open what is left of the Duke's home as a tea house for interested visitors as a way to satisfy curiosity about the place. This would also allow them to operate the ranch without the public interfering with day-to-day ranching.

Lynn serves both lunch and afternoon tea for members of the public, and delivers informal talks on the ranch's history.

A DOUBLE DREAM RANCH

In 1984, the first weekend the Cartwrights opened the tea house, over 500 people came in three days. Lynn was astonished at the turnout.

"It was a disaster," Lynn says. "But we knew we had something that was going to go." With the help of a friend, and her mother who was visiting, Lynn made baked goods for her guests. Though John and Lynn have divorced, Lynn continues to run her tea house as a business.

She is still remodeling the house to approximate the home that Prince Edward owned. She is even restoring the garden from original seed stock. Fortunately, because she has excellent photographs portraying the place as it once was, Lynn has been able to refer to the photos in her restoration work.

She tries to keep the place open from spring until fall. Except when the ranch weans calves or does other ranch work that requires concentrated attention, the Cartwrights keep the ranch gates open for visitors.

Lynn serves her hungry guests hearty fare, including homemade buns, a vegetable tray and Prince of Wales Cake.

"We always have to have Prince of Wales Cake," she says. "The mountain water also makes great coffee. People really seem to love the coffee."

Folks in private cars, on bus tours and in school groups flock to the ranch. Lynn thinks people love to visit the EP because they are participating in a dream.

"There are two dreams," she says. "One of the Prince and his royal family, and the other dream is of the cowboy and the lifestyle of the cowboy...when people come to the ranch, they are coming to a fantasy." Lynn still expresses surprise that people want to stay, talk, visit and learn all they can about the ranch and its history. She has great plans for future restoration and more history presentations. Meanwhile, hungry readers can share in this royal history by sampling Lynn's Prince of Wales Cake.

Prince of Wales Cake

2 cups raisins

2 to 2½ cups water

1 cup vegetable oil

2 cups brown sugar

2 eggs

1 tablespoon vanilla

2½ cups all-purpose flour

2 tablespoons baking soda

1 tablespoon baking powder

2 tablespoons ground cinnamon

2 tablespoons ground nutmeg

1 tablespoon salt

Simmer the raisins in the water for 10 minutes. Cool and drain, and save the liquid.

Mix together the oil, sugar, eggs and vanilla. Add 1¾ cups of the water that the raisins have been simmered in.

Sift the dry ingredients together. Add to the first mixture and stir well. Fold in the raisins.

Pour into a 9" x 13" baking pan, oiled and floured. Bake about 40 minutes at 350 degrees F. Ice with frosting of your choice.

McIntyre Ranch
McGrath, Alberta

Where the deer and antelope play
Opal Walker, Canadian Ranch Cook

What first appears to be livestock out on the range at the McIntyre Ranch soon proves to be a few antelope and herds of mule and white-tail deer (some 1,200 of them), mingling with the cattle. Above, all kinds of game birds fly through deep-blue skies over the rolling hills covered with tall grass—all of which makes the McIntyre seem the ideal western ranch that is almost Hollywood-movie perfect.

Long-time foreman David Walker rides herd on this 10-section cow/calf operation. And David's wife Opal runs the kitchen. They've been married for over 35 years, and both come from farm and ranch backgrounds in Saskatchewan, some 75 miles south of Regina.

Following their marriage, they worked on a number of Canadian ranches before settling at the McIntyre in June, 1978.

Owned by the Thrall family since 1947, this 6,400-acre spread runs nearly 4,500 cattle, including a herd of registered Herefords.

But, as with so many other ranches that raise breeding stock, the McIntyre has a cross-breeding program that includes the introduction of some Red Angus to the herd. Until about 1983, the ranch also had a farming division growing wheat and other grains.

It's a given that cowboys have traditionally looked down on farmers, so these old attitudes created some fun at the McIntyre. On some ranches cowboys won't even eat with farm crews. Such animosity has never been that deep-seated here, though farmers eat on one side of the table and cowboys sit on the other side. The old rivalry does make for some good-natured ribbing, but everybody seems to get along just fine.

"Hasn't it always been like that?" cook Opal Walker asks in reference to the traditional rivalry between cowboys and farmers.

Young Cowboys and Wannabes

Like many ranch cooks on large spreads, Opal didn't particularly want the cook's job. She had been on other ranches with David without cooking for the crews. When the Walkers arrived, the McIntyre Ranch needed a cook, and Opal agreed to take the position, but only for a while, just to fill in until a permanent cook was hired...that was more than 10 years ago.

Opal does get some time off, though, because the cookhouse stays open only from March until November. With a warm laugh, Opal says her biggest problem in the cookhouse is just getting tired.

During winter months when the cowboy crew gets smaller, the ranch hires only married hands. The McIntyre has many comfortable houses right on the ranch for these couples. David and the McIntyre owners each year hope that the cowboys' wives will feed them well to get them through the winter. If winter brings unusually bad weather, the ranch hires more cowboys and Opal opens the cookhouse to feed the extra help. She usually opens the kitchen in early spring, though, cooking for about 20 hands.

Most of the cowboys are under 30, and Opal says hiring older cowboys who are set in their ways presents difficulties, as they are not flexible enough to change. Because of legal restrictions, cowboys at the McIntyre are all Canadians. They bring their own saddles and tack, and better know how to ride and rope well. When hiring new cowboys, she says she can pick up the phone, talk to them for five minutes and know if they will work out or not.

"You get some of these wanna-be cowboys who have never done the work before, and you have to give them a chance...we've given some a chance and some have worked out," she says. The ranch also allows wives to ride with their husbands, and they have even hired some women.

Cowboys at the McIntyre do lots of riding, but they also have to work off of their horses to do chores like repairing fences. "The guys who only want to do horseback work don't get jobs here," Opal stresses.

Horses still provide the primary form of transportation at the ranch, which owns a band of about 50-60 horses and used to raise its own foals each year. Until a couple of years ago, the ranch even fed livestock using a horse-drawn team.

Recently they sold their team, because winters have been mild, and with good range management they've been able to set aside enough winter pasturage so that they usually have to do only a month's winter feeding. The Alberta winds blow the winter range clear and the grass is in excellent shape under the snow. The ranch owns its own feedlot, and calves in the feedlot, receive regular feeding during the winter months. From March to May, calving takes place; branding occurs in June.

STILL A BUSINESS

Unlike many outfits, the McIntyre keeps calves over the winter and sells them when prices are highest. Owning their own feedlot means no pressure to move cattle out as regularly as on ranches where cattle are sold from the range to a feedlot. McIntyre calves put on weight right at home. With good pasture, the ranch isn't as much at the mercy of cattle auctions that handle most of the sales for smaller ranchers, who must sell periodically to maintain a positive cash flow.

Despite the romance associated with ranching, it is still first and foremost a business. On large outfits like the McIntyre, managers must spend a greater portion of their time in the office. David Walker holds meetings with the owners to set up cattle sales, and he meets regularly with accountants and everybody else involved in ranch economics. He has to travel 32 miles each way from ranch headquarters to the main office in Lethbridge.

Even though she became a cook by default, Opal still finds pleasure in cooking for the crews who don't complain and like their fare simple and direct—just meat, potatoes, vegetables...and dessert.

"We don't cook anything fancy," Opal says. Despite many stories about cowboys with a sweet tooth, Opal says that the punchers on the McIntyre really don't want sweets for every meal, though one old cowboy who worked at the ranch for over 20 years did favor desserts.

Opal learned to cook from her mother. One of 14 children, Opal, like her brothers and sisters, worked on the Saskatchewan family farm. Opal had six children who are all grown now, so cooking for large groups is in her blood.

Opal enjoys cooking two of her mother's favorite dishes, apple pie and clam chowder.

"I make it just like she made it—with fresh apples," she says of her pie. Many of her dishes she says she just throws together. Only a ranch cook with confidence and skill can make such a claim.

Opal's Apple Pie

1 pie crust, your own recipe for a double crust pie
2 tablespoons flour
5 to 6 cups fresh MacIntosh apples, cored and sliced
1 tablespoon sugar
¾ cup and 1 tablespoon white sugar
1 teaspoon ground cinnamon
1 tablespoon butter
1 egg (beaten)

Mix 1 tablespoon flour with 1 tablespoon sugar and sprinkle in the bottom of the crust.

Fill the crust with the fresh apples and add the remaining sugar. Sprinkle the remaining flour and cinnamon over the apples and add the butter.

Cover with the top pie crust and brush with the beaten egg.

Bake at 400 degrees F. for 15 minutes, reduce the heat to 350 degrees F. and bake for an additional 45 minutes.

LONGVIEW
ALBERTA, CANADA

Gaile Gallup, Cowboy Bachelor Cook

Whether wandering the hot desert sands of the Southwest under deep blue clear skies, or riding through cool mountains and streams of the Canadian Rockies, the cowboy has always been considered the lone knight of the range, the solitary warrior, the heroic fighter for justice and individual rights, representative of the new lands of the West.

Just across the border from Alberta in Montana, cowboy artist Charles M. Russell has assumed the status of a legend.

As Canadian songwriter and cowboy Ian Tyson has written in a song that pays tribute to Russell, he captured all the glory and beauty of the cowboy and his world.

Even today, cowboys and non-cowboys alike often shape their images of the West from what they have seen in the canvases of Charlie Russell and his followers. Rare is the bunkhouse or ranch house without a Russell reproduction hanging on a wall. Sometimes faded, some ragged around the edges, or hung in fancy frames, these pictures have become the definitive image of the cowboys, Indians and life on the North American frontier. A working cowboy, Russell knew his subject matter about as well as any artist of his time.

Up in Canada on the lush east slope of the Rockies, where summer meadows rise to meet tree-covered hills, a canyon road through the Highwood and Livingstone mountains from the famous resort of Banff leads to the Longview-High River country. Riding for outfits in these areas, such as the 17,000-acre OH and the Y CROSS, modern cowboy artist

Gaile Gallup is the living embodiment of the Russell tradition, portraying the cowboy life he knows and loves.

Gaile's family has always ranched. His grandfather and uncle were Canadian cowboys, and before moving to the Longview area, they ranched in southeast Alberta. In the late 1930s and early 1940s Gaile's family moved north to the western side of the province where they ran a small operation with 120 head of Herefords.

Since he grew up around horses and cattle, Gaile decided the cowboy life was the only life for him.

"Through high school I wasn't much of a student. All I could think about was looking back at these hills and wanting to cowboy. So I quit school in the 12th grade and went to work on the ranches," Gaile says.

He's even cowboyed some in the United States down by Roundup, Montana, in the central part of the state. He doesn't see much difference between Canadian and U.S. cowboys.

But after a few years punching cows, Gaile felt a need to do something more with his life. He wanted to chase another boyhood dream; Gaile Gallup wanted to be an artist.

Even as a kid he had sketched. And he had actually sold a few pieces to neighbors and friends. He knew Russell's work and he used to copy the artist's sketches and study his paintings. "When I was younger, he was sort of a hero to me," Gallup says, and he still considers Russell to be the best Western artist.

As a budding artist, Gaile visited museums in Helena and Great Falls, Montana where outstanding Russell collections hang. Being a young man of conviction and determination, Gaile Gallup entered the Alberta College of Art in Calgary in 1976 and started to draw and paint those things which had always intrigued him—cowboys, horses and cattle. He spent two years in art school developing and perfecting his talents.

His work focuses on contemporary cowboys and ranch life. He depicts today's West, not the frontier of a hundred years ago. He says he can't see any point in painting over what has already been done.

Gaile pictures the real everyday activities of cowboy life—cowboys on horseback roping calves, a gather of steers, a remuda. Because of his cowboy experience, he feels he's a better artist and more prepared to accomplish his long-time goal.

He says that to portray the cowboy life with any kind of feeling or honesty, an artist has to live the life. Russell probably would have been proud of Gaile Gallup.

Traditional in its realism and accurate in detail, Gallup's work shows what a working cowboy knows, such as a particular type of saddle, exactly how a rope is coiled, how steers act in a gather, how a cow and calf react to one another in a variety of circumstances. And he better be accurate, because some of his toughest critics are fellow cowboys.

Located in the small ranching community of Longview, Alberta, southwest of Calgary, Gaile's house is part studio, part bachelor quarters, sitting up on a hill with big windows overlooking the town, with a wonderful view of the foothills and the Canadian Rockies to the west.

Bachelor cowboys are nothing new. Back in the heyday of ranching and the range cowboy, many punchers for short periods wanted to escape the bunkhouse and avoid steady work. They wanted to take jobs for just a month of so. They could always get work at roundups and brandings, or wait until fall when cattle had to be trailed from the range to railroad loading pens, where they were shipped to feedlots or slaughterhouses, usually in the Midwest.

Bachelor cowboys sometimes took jobs at line shacks out on the range by themselves with their strings of horses and maybe a dog. When wagons came in from headquarters to deliver supplies, or when a rider or two stopped by as they drifted through the country, these bachelor cowboys had their only company.

Line cabins were pretty primitive and lonely, but depending on the cowboy, they were often good escapes from the pressures of encroaching civilization, or places to gather one's thoughts.

As on every part of a ranch, out on the range the bachelor cowboy had plenty of work to do. He had to check windmills and water holes, keep the cattle on the right range, and make sure that predators gave a wide berth to new calves. Fences, if there were fences on his range, always needed repair, and he had to gather firewood to keep his wood stove aglow.

As one old cowboy reportedly said, "Anybody who does this kind of work has to be comfortable with his own company."

Now Gaile Gallup doesn't exactly live this kind of life. He gets around pretty easily in his pickup, and friends come over to visit. But he's a good enough cowboy to get work when he wants, and to devote time to his art when he wants to create. The country around Longview, with its big ranches, foothill scenery and mountains reaching above 10,000 feet, provides him lots of inspiration.

Though he makes a good living from his art, Gaile doesn't want to give up cowboying. Sitting in his studio all winter doing art work makes him anxious to get out and work the range come each spring.

As bachelor cowboys have always done, Gaile cooks for himself. "I like roast beef and potatoes...pretty basic stuff and typical cowboy fare," Gaile laughs, as he describes his kitchen skills. But like many a bachelor cowboy, he has a few dishes of which he's proud. One of these dishes is his delectable chicken wings that he likes to prepare when his cowboy and artist friends drop over to visit during those long and cold Alberta winters. Under similar circumstances, what dishes might Charlie Russell have served to his friends during the dark, freezing Montana winters?

Gaile Gallup's Bachelor Chicken Wings

1½ cups honey
2 pounds of chicken wings
3 tablespoons vegetable oil
½ cup catsup
½ cup vinegar
dash soy sauce

Heat the oil and brown the chicken wings in frying pan. Remove the wings and place in a pot.

Combine the honey, catsup, vinegar and soy sauce. Pour over the chicken, cover, and simmer over slow heat for about ½ hour. Remove and serve over rice.

Serves: 4 to 6

THE TYSON RANCH
LONGVIEW, ALBERTA, CANADA

WHERE SHOW BUSINESS AND RANCHING MEET
Twylla Tyson, Cook

The worlds of ranching and show business appear to be miles apart, but up in the ranch country of western Alberta, nestled comfortably in the foothills just south of Calgary, the two worlds come together.

Home to cowboy musician Ian Tyson, his wife Twylla and their young daughter Adelita, the Tyson ranch produces fine cutting horses. Cowboy songs and great food add to the richness of the Tysons' life.

From their living room, where shelves are stuffed with books and records, to Twylla's spacious, practical kitchen, the Tysons fill their home with music and talk of fine horses. From their window a viewer can see the Tysons' barn and corral, where some of the finest cutting horses in Canada are waiting for their next competition.

Horses and cattle used for cutting practice provide part of the focus at the ranch, the Tysons' home for more than 10 years. Doc's Summer Wages, their stallion, leads the horse herd, and has been instrumental in allowing the Tysons to raise champion cutting horses.

MAKINGS OF A CHAMPION CUTTER

The sport of cutting has come a long way from the days when a cowboy pushed his pony into a herd of cattle and cut out cows he wanted to isolate. In those bygone days before fast pickups and specialized horses, cowboys used the same horse to fix

Twylla Tyson getting ready for a winter cutting practice on her Canadian Ranch.

fences, chase wolves, round up cattle and even go to town on Saturday night.

Somewhere along the line, cowmen found certain horses worked cows better than others. As cowboys say, some horses have more cow in them. So when horse and rider had to move in, select cows that had to be cut away from the main herd and ease them over to an area away from the other cattle, those horses that took to the work naturally were selected for this demanding task. Early-day longhorns were not wearing those horns for decoration. Those cutting horses had to be tough.

With its origin as an exhibition event at some big rodeos, the sport of cutting has grown over time. Registered quarter horses almost always make the best cutting horses; they are bred for intelligence, quick reaction and cow sense. Cutting aficionados know the top cutting bloodlines, like Doc Bar and Mr. San Peppy.

By 1940, when the quarter horse had become an established breed, rules for cutting contests were formulated, and in 1946, enthusiasts organized the National Cutting Horse Association. Now cutting has become a major sport, with hundreds of thousands of dollars awarded in prize money each year. Cowboys always keep their eyes peeled to spot that horse with the extra bit of cow in it, so they can begin the years of training that make a champion.

COWBOYOGRAPHY

Twylla grew up in Rosebud, northeast of Calgary, just south of Drumheller, where her father ran a grain elevator and her mother taught school. She learned about horses, and especially cutting horses, from Ian, whom she met in Calgary.

Ian grew up in British Columbia on a small farm and he put in a stint as a bareback bronc rider on the rodeo circuit. Eventually he headed east to art school in Toronto, and while there, he worked as a commercial artist and sometimes folk singer.

In the early 1960s his musical career took off when he teamed up with Sylvia Fricker to form Ian and Sylvia, a very popular folk singing duet. Ian wrote such songs as "Four Strong Winds" and "Someday Soon" that became classics, but after many successful years, the duo and Ian and Sylvia's marriage broke up.

Ian has been involved with horses and cutting competitions for a long time. He served on the Board of Directors of the Canadian Cutting Horse Association and he and Twylla both compete.

Ian's fascination with the sport has affected his music. "The Steeldust Line" from his 1989 album "I Outgrew the Wagon" is a story about traveling in winter from Alberta to Las Vegas, Nevada to compete in a cutting. The song, along with all his recent music, is popular because Ian sings about the realities of cowboy life in a way few other musicians understand. Twylla is Ian's toughest and most perceptive critic.

Because of the demands his musical career makes on their lives, the Tysons have to balance their time so that they get all their ranch chores done, make concert dates and still have time for their daughter, Adelita.

Several years ago the Tysons decided to record Ian's two new solo cowboy song albums, "Old Corrals and Sagebrush" and "Ian Tyson," in the basement of their spacious ranch home. Bringing in six musicians and recording technicians created havoc, but Twylla organized the event and managed to feed everyone. They recorded one album in 1982 and the second in January and February, 1984. They sure had worked the bugs out of the recording process.

Today these two albums and two more, "Cowboyography" and "I Outgrew the Wagon," have become cowboy music classics.

Cowboy songs have all but disappeared from the radio, but because of Ian's contribution to the restoration of this uniquely North American art form, as a friend has said, "Ian should be awarded the All-Around Buckle for songwriting."

Pop stations don't seem to show an interest in Ian's music, and so-called country stations actually play more Nashville and hillbilly music than they do real cowboy music, despite the fact that many C&W stars wear big cowboy hats.

At least in Canada, "Cowboyography" received some deserved recognition when the album was awarded top honors as Best Album, and the song "Navajo Rug" was voted Best Single. Air time for cowboy music here in the United States is unfortunately lacking, and there are no true Western music stations in this country. Today, Ian, together with the Sons of the Pioneers, Hi Busse and the Frontiersmen, Red Stegall, Chris LeDoux, Gary McMahan, Don Edwards and even Riders in the Sky, are among many who keep this unique music alive.

TWYLLA'S KITCHEN SENSE

Maybe having kitchen sense is like a horse that has cow in his blood—just part of the natural order for a cook. Cooking comes naturally for her, says Twylla. She cooked at home as a youngster but never thought of it as a big deal. Her kitchen skills just seemed to be at hand when she needed them.

Today Twylla is known among the Tysons' cowboy and music friends as a fine cook, and the Tyson ranch has become famous as a good place to stop for that special meal.

Despite their hectic schedules, Ian and Twylla work well together to maintain their ranch, train and practice on their top quarter horses, and still travel to the many cuttings. As anyone who has ever had to trailer a horse for ranch work, or to travel to a rodeo or horse show knows, travel time is demanding and filled with unexpected adventure.

Ian Tyson cutting cattle at the Tyson Ranch.

15

But when she's at home, Twylla loves to cook up a real Western specialty, her venison chili, with mouth-watering feta cheese, sour cream and hot sauce topping, that has her guests exclaiming the virtues of real ranch cooking.

Tyson Ranch Chili

1 12-ounce can beef consomme

1½ cups red wine

½ - ¾ can tomato sauce

2 bay leaves

4 cinnamon sticks

pinch of ground coriander

1 tablespoon dried oregano

2 to 3 tablespoons vegetable oil

4 cloves garlic, chopped

4 to 5 venison steaks cut into bite-sized cubes

(beef may be substituted for venison)

1 large onion, chopped

1 green bell pepper, stem and seeds removed, chopped

1 red bell pepper, stem and seeds removed, chopped

1 can green chile peppers, chopped

2 to 3 Jalapeño chiles, stems and seeds removed, chopped

6 to 8 large dried apricots, chopped

Cooked fettucine noodles

Feta cheese

Sour cream

Hot sauce

Combine the consomme, wine, tomato sauce, bay leaves, cinnamon, coriander, and oregano in a large pot.

Heat the oil in pan until hot. Add the garlic and meat and brown. Remove and put into the cooking pot. Add the onion, green pepper, and red pepper to the oil and saute for 1-2 minutes. Add to the pot. Add the chiles and apricots to the mixture and simmer for 2 hours. Turn off the heat and let stand for 1 hour. Reheat before serving.

Serve on top of fettucine noodles and topped with feta cheese, sour cream, and hot sauce. All three go on at once.

Serves: 4 to 6.

SECTION II:
HEART OF THE ROCKIES

The old-time ranch hand wasn't exactly topheavy with worldly
goods. His horse gear, a bedroll, and a warbag—as a rule, a
seamless sack holding a few clothes—was about all, and in
total was always spoken of as, "my forty years' gatherin's"——

Spike Van Cleve
40 Years' Gatherin's
The Lowell Press, 1977

17

Of all the states we explored in interviewing our ranch cooks, Montana, Wyoming and Colorado feel most like home. When we started this project, we both lived in Montana's wild, scenic Bitterroot Valley.

We've cowboyed a lot in all three states. Tom had packed into the high Rockies regularly, and Joel had rodeoed across both prairies and high peaks in our home range.

We met so many ranchers all over the West that we had a hard time selecting the kind of ranches we wanted to visit. Anyone who thinks ranching and the cowboy way of life are disappearing has never visited Montana, Wyoming and Colorado.

Large corporate ranches managed with an eye for profits, and smaller family spreads run by mom, pop and the kids dot the rolling, grassy plains to the east and nestle in the spectacular white-capped mountain ranges and lush valleys in the western part of these states. Anyone unfamiliar with this rugged land or who thinks a two-acre plot is an estate will probably find the Rockies overwhelming. Here in the West, folks talk as easily about a section (640 acres, or a square mile) as people back East talk about an acre. This is Big Country!

In 1885, a joker wrote in the Colorado Springs Gazette that some Colorado ranchers had acquired a telescope from Cambridge, Massachusetts so powerful that during annual roundup, they would be able to read cattle brands from 150 miles away.

This country boasts a history as long and proud as the land is big. The ranchers, bosses, cowboys, and of course, the cooks share in a life rich with tradition, based on honest, hard outdoor work, a love of and respect for the land, a pride in family, and an ongoing sense of rugged individualism—those values long associated with the American frontier. A rugged land builds tough people.

In winter blizzards, temperatures sometimes drop to 50 degrees below zero with wind chills of 80 below, and in summer, the sun in a cloudless sky will blister the flesh right off your bones. We can't count the number of times we've saddled up, often twice a day, to feed stock in weather as tough as nails.

There are no tomorrows in ranch country. The work's done each day, seven days a week. So meals are mighty important to cowboys and cowgirls, and a cook is a person of consequence out on the range.

Some parts of the Rocky Mountain states are frozen in time. From flat sagebrush plateaus that go on for miles to parklands below jagged peaks that tower over green valleys, this landscape resembles country seen by Lewis and Clark and painted by the great nineteenth-century Western painters, Charles Russell, Frederic Remington and Thomas Moran, who helped create the romantic vision of the West with its cowboys, its weather and its open land.

In visiting these ranches and talking to the folks, we saw this romantic vision has real substance. Nowhere was this romance in the flesh more true than when we sat down in the kitchens of cooks such as Vera Springs at the Flying D and Mary Noyes at the Shelton Ranch and talked about cowboying, or when we jawed with former cowboy and now cook Jim Snead at the Lyons Ranch, or when we set a spell with Sheila Whitlock at the Pitchfork, a ranch in Meeteetse, Wyoming made known by cowboy photographer Charles Belden.

In cowboy country, ranchers keep a wary eye on the early morning farm report, check cattle prices, worry about the rain or lack thereof, and pray for winter snow in the high country so there will be summer irrigation water. Then they turn around and worry that the coming snows may endanger their herds. And yes, these cowboys and ranchers still hang out at the local feedstore to catch up on gossip. Some say modern progress simply passed these places by, or is this country, where time seems to stand still, really the last bastion against the increasing depersonalization of our age?

The rest of America may have undergone some astounding changes since World War II, but in Rocky Mountain ranch country, through their manner of speech, dress and work, cowboys are the descendants of those Texas cowpunchers who wandered up the trails through the open range in the late 1800s, working for a dollar a day. Maybe because of this sense of continuity, we cherish this way of life. Cowboys still work cattle from the back of a horse. They still calve in wet, cold springs, round up herds in foul Rocky Mountain blizzards, and still find time to train horses.

Just as in the old days, nowhere else provides more of a focus for cowboys than the ranch cookhouse. Whether they're old stove-up cowboys, cowboy wives or newcomers eager to taste the real life of the West, cooks play a pivotal role in ranch life on spreads large or small. Woe to the cook who hasn't prepared his vittles on time for a crew just in after a day branding or gathering horses and cattle in the high country. These cowboys are hungry, but they'd better show due respect to the cook, too. No wearing spurs into the cookhouse, and they'd better watch their language and mind their manners lest they incur the cook's wrath. As many of our cooks told us, the cookhouse is their domain, and they still rule their kingdom with a tight rein.

Marsha Spencer at the Big Horn Ranch, Cowdrey, Colorado (see next page).

CHAPTER TWO
COLORADO

BIG HORN RANCH
COWDREY, COLORADO

COWTIME AT THE BIG HORN RANCH
A Visit with Ranch Cook Marsha Spencer

Cowdrey is little more than a wide spot on Colorado Highway 125, north of the Jackson County seat of Walden and south of the Wyoming border. Cowdrey boasts a general store/post office, gas pumps and little else. Ranchers and cowboys drive across the 8,200-foot-high North Park Basin to Cowdrey to buy tack, tools, hardware, gas, gloves and groceries.

According to Marty Hanson, wife of Big Horn Ranch manager Cleyborn "Ceeb" Hanson, Cowdrey got its name from a local family of the same name who settled the area in about 1890.

About two miles west of town, down a dusty gravel road, the Big Horn Ranch headquarters sits hard by the North Platte River.

The Platte and its many tributaries drain the North Park Basin, bounded by the Medicine Bow Mountains 13 miles to the east and the Park Range, with the Continental Divide to the west.

Made up of three ranches, the Big Horn is a huge spread, running many head of Herefords, Angus, Black Baldies and hybrid commercial cattle. The Hansons typify many ranchers who do not care to discuss number of acres, or numbers of cattle. They consider the question crass, much like asking a businessman how much money he takes to the bank. Beef consumers today seem to show a preference for cross-bred cattle, and that's what the Big Horn tries to provide for the market. Big Horn headquarters includes a manager's house, a bunkhouse, a large, two-story barn, and a two-story cook's residence and mess hall where the cowboys and hands eat. The clapboard white buildings with red trim are situated in a semicircle that forms a natural barrier to stiff winds that sweep up through North Park during winter and spring.

A few old cottonwoods towering among the buildings give the headquarters a sheltered, homey look that is a comfort to all who live and work at the ranch. The visitor, approaching the Big Horn, travels back a hundred years or more into the past, when cattle ranches dominated the old western landscape. Here, a different sense of time presides, just as it did in those old days that seem to live even now at the Big Horn.

Ranch cook Marsha Spencer doesn't believe in daylight savings. Like many a ranch cook, she trusts the natural cycles that determine the daily round of chores in cattle country, rather than time artificially imposed by government bureaucrats in some far-away office. The land, the weather, the seasons, and of course, the cattle tell ranchers more of what they need to know in order to survive.

"Seems like they're always messing with the clocks. I just can't keep up with it. Around here we stay on cowtime," says Marsha. "That's breakfast before daylight, dinner when the sun is straight up and supper when the sun goes down." Marsha controls her kitchen clocks with the same authority she exercises in bossing the cowpunchers and ranch hands who eat at her table.

Tall and thin, Marsha possesses a quick smile and long, blond hair she brushes out of her face as she works in the confines of her overheated ranch kitchen. Well-lit and clean, her kitchen is dominated by a white enamel stove in the southwest corner, and southwest windows that give her a clear view of the winding Platte and wide, flat acres of natural grassland lying between the river and the Mount Zirkel Wilderness 13 miles away.

A single mother of three and a surrogate mom for the dozen cowboys and hay pitchers on the Big Horn, Marsha learned early to be firm. She remembers one of the first lessons of her childhood was learned when her grandfather gave her first horse to her.

BRONCBUSTIN' COOK

"My granddaddy gave me the meanest mare he could find," Marsha recalls. "He told me if I could break her, she was mine. He wanted me to be tough." She gentled that horse and she learned to be self-reliant, just as her granddad had intended, but even to this day she doesn't like mares. Marsha learned many a lesson from her grandparents, who hold a special place in her heart.

Born in the high mountain town of Durango in southern Colorado, she soon moved with her grandfolks to Aztec, just across the New Mexico border. Marsha's grandmother had suffered a fatal stroke, and her parents thought it best for her Grandpa if she went to live with him and took over household chores for a while.

"Grandpa always had horses, and I rode every chance I got," Marsha says. "In Aztec there ain't a helluva lot else to do."

Alone with her grandfather, Marsha found herself having to learn how to cook as best she could, with neither her mother nor her grandmother to help her. Sometimes her experiments succeeded, but she also had her failures. She remembers her first disaster.

"I didn't know diddly about a roast, but Grandpa wanted me to cook one. I had watched Grandma tenderize steaks, and I thought that was what you were supposed to do with all meat. Well, I was a-pounding away on this big roast with a hammer. Grandpa came home and he almost died when he saw what I was doing."

On another occasion it was Marsha who almost did the dying. She was just beginning to learn the basics of meal preparation when one day her grandfather came into the kitchen.

"Here you go, girl," her granddad said, "cook this." He flopped a huge cow tongue down on the kitchen table.

"I damn near fainted," Marsha says.

Without her grandmother's cookbooks, Marsha says, she would have been lost. "Anytime I had a problem in the kitchen, I'd pull out one of Grandma's cookbooks."

After her 81-year-old grandfather died of a heart attack, Marsha moved to Judd's Dude Ranch just north of the Mogollon Rim country near Aripine, Arizona. Marsha cleaned cabins and cooked for the manager, his family and the hired hands.

"Now that was really big-time cooking," Marsha says. "I learned a helluva lot in a helluva big hurry. I started a roast or a pie and then I had to run out to clean cabins. Then, lo and behold, I forgot the wax paper under the pie crust. Pretty soon I smelled something burning and I blasted back over to the kitchen to a stinking mess in my oven. Seems like that whole four years at Judd's I was always on the run, but that's how I learned how to plan my supplies, my cooking and my menus ahead so I could cook with care."

BANTY HEN WITH A BROOD OF CHICKS

In about 1984 Marsha moved back to Colorado because she missed the pine-clad high country and the snow-capped peaks of her native state. Some ponderosas grew in the Apache Forest near where she lived when she was in Aripine, but Marsha yearned for the spruce, Douglas fir and colorful tamaracks of Colorado.

Now at the Big Horn she can glance out her living room window to the east and see the Medicine Bow Mountains. From her kitchen window, 22 miles to the west she can see the 13,000-foot-high-ridge of the Park Range as it runs to Rabbit Ears Pass and to Steamboat Springs beyond. Out her window Marsha can also contemplate her favorite stand of willows growing along the banks of the North Platte as it meanders a few yards from the house.

"Depending on the season, the river either runs brown with mud or white with ice," Marsha says, as she describes the two major times of the year that pose her the greatest challenge.

Summer means haying season, and Marsha must deal with an additional 30 to 40 hungry cowboys besides the six or seven regular hands she usually tends. All that extra help keeps her on the run.

"The three ranches under the Big Horn brand take up a lot of country, so during haying, the crews seem scattered to the four corners," Marsha says. "I pack lunches out to them so they don't have to knock off and come to the cookhouse. Sometimes it gets a little hectic, but you just have to cowboy up and get 'er done."

Winter lasts about six months at 8,200 feet, and those who live and work at the Big Horn must be prepared to take the worst.

"It gets down to 55 below zero sometimes and the wind blows hard enough to whip the hair off a dog. That's when it's nice to be the ranch cook. I get to sit by the stove and spit on the fire while the guys are out feeding cattle, looking after the horses and breaking ice off the water holes so's the stock can drink." For Marsha, driving her kids to catch the school bus, and sometimes to school functions 12 miles away in Walden, can be the worst part of winter.

YOU DON'T MESS WITH THE COOK

"When it's 50 below, that old car seat feels like you're sitting on a chunk of ice," Marsha says.

But despite frantic haying seasons and frigid, blustering winters, Marsha loves her life on the Big Horn. She watches over the bachelor cowboys and hands on her ranch like a banty hen brooding over her chicks. She works from sunup to sundown seven days a week with no time off for holidays or weekends except for her one-week vacation and New Year's day, which she usually takes off. Around Christmas season, when things traditionally slow down at the ranch, she still stays on and prepares a huge holiday dinner for all the hands, despite the fact ranch owner A.G. Davis schedules her for her time off during this season. Marsha knows that Christmas dinner is mighty important to her cowboys.

"The Big Horn is the only home these boys have, and if I don't stay and fix dinner for them, they won't have a Christmas. So I stick on and take care of them," she says.

The cowboys watch over her too, even though she has to take a lot of horseplay from them. She still maintains a proper distance and keeps her dignity. Occasionally decorum falls by the wayside, though. She remembers one time when she made cream puffs and forgot to put out napkins for the grateful crew.

"No one said a word, but they made the biggest mess you ever saw. The boss (Ceeb) had cream all over his face, and he tried to wipe it off on my dresstail. No way, Jose. You don't mess with the cook; that's fire in the fences."

Ranch owner A.G. Davis owns the Winn-Dixie grocery store chain located in several eastern states, and doesn't get out to Colorado as much as he would like, but when he is at the Big Horn looking over his cattle, he spends as much time as he can in the saddle.

"Mr. Davis is a fine man, and he stays on a horse just about all the time he's here," comments Marsha. When he checks the cattle, looks in on the haying, and watches the irrigation, Marsha always packs him a big lunch.

But Davis, unlike some of the hands, never fusses about the fare he gets on his visits to the Big Horn. Marsha also likes to coddle her crew, and she bakes frequently and prepares a new dessert each day to keep those hungry hands happy.

"Why, some of these guys want steak or roast for every meal," Marsha says, "but I figure there's more to life than just meat. I feed 'em what I think they should be eating, and I still keep it basic. Those boys have to get a balanced diet, and I'm here to see that they do."

Marsha Spencer's Fresh Apple Cake For Happy Crews

Mix:

2 cups sugar

1 cup vegetable oil

2 eggs

Add:

1 cup pecans, chopped

3 cups fresh apples, diced or sliced

1 teaspoon vanilla

Mix together:

3 cups all-purpose flour

½ tablespoon salt

1 tablespoon ground cinnamon

1 tablespoon baking soda

Mix all the ingredients together and pour into a greased and floured pan. Bake at 300 degrees F. 1½ to 2 hours or until done.

Burr Ranch
Walden, Colorado

A Moose in the Yard
Charollette Sanches, Cook

About eight miles south of Walden, Colorado, the headquarters of the Burr Ranch perches along the wide Illinois River flood plain. Third generation co-owner Bob Burr says the ranch was established before the turn of the century by a family named Monroe, about whom he knows nothing more. Burr's grandfather, Doc Jones, obtained the place in the 1920s and held onto the property until Bob's father, Clarence Burr, took over.

"My dad came up here during the Depression and started running the ranch. It was a tough son-of-a-gun trying to make a living back in them days, but Dad was tough too, and somehow he survived and prospered. We (the three Burr brothers) ended up with a pretty nice spread, and we're able—with a lot of hard work—to still make a living at ranching. It ain't an easy life by any stretch of the imagination, but it's a good life."

Like the ranch itself, Burr Ranch headquarters blends the new and old in an improbable but practical combination. Cowboys sleep in the 100-year-old log bunkhouse. Nearby, a small log blacksmith shop and tack room is also a century old, but a mobile home houses the cook shack and dining room. While hay is put up with the latest baling and stacking equipment, horse-drawn sleds are used to feed the cattle in the winter.

Native grass grows right up to the buildings of the headquarters compound, sheltered by a ring of willow trees that offers occasional protection to moose and other smaller wildlife. "Moose in the yard!" is a common warning around here, signalling just who has the right of way.

Cooking Just Came Natural

Like many a rancher, Bob won't say just how many acres are under the Burr brand, but the ranch is big enough to keep him, his brother Bill and a full-time crew of five busy year-round. A psychiatrist in Tucson, Bob's brother John escapes to the ranch when he can, but Bob and Bill really run the outfit.

The old intermountain glacial basin, now called North Park, forms a bowl about 33 miles long and 30 miles wide. Rimmed by the Park Range to the west, the Medicine Bow Mountains to the east and Rabbit Ears Mountains to the south, this catchment basin collects the headwaters of the North Platte River in the form of the Michigan, Illinois, Canadian and Grizzly River tributaries that join in the north end of the park and flow into Wyoming. The surrounding peaks, many over 9,000 feet, trap snowfall in winter and spring that melts during summer and fall.

Because of plentiful water, North Park provides a perfect location to grow hay, raise cattle and run a ranch. Flood waters irrigate Bob's meadows, growing lots of natural native grass.

"You can't beat natural grass for producing beef," Bob says. "Grass-fed beef is some of the sweetest meat you'll ever sink a tooth into."

When we interviewed Charollette Sanches, she had been cooking at the Burr Ranch for five years. She was raised on a farm near Grand Junction, Colorado where her folks ran a few sheep. Charollette says her parents got carried away when they gave her unusual name to her.

"They didn't know when to stop with the spelling," she says. Her parents' farm had the usual milk cows, horses and pigs, and Charollette grew up with her share of the chores. "You know, there's always something to be done on a farm or ranch." Her mother had a job to help pay bills. Charollette, her brother and sister had to pick up the slack at home. "I had to fix most of our meals when I was just a little kid," she says. "Cooking just came natural to me."

By sixteen, Charollette also worked at a job to help support the family farm. "I worked at a preschool center, and there I learned to cook for groups. It was a good education. I probably learned a lot more at that school than the kids did."

After school, Charollette married a young cowboy, and he got a job at the Burr Ranch, where they moved. "We came here as a team. He was to cowboy and I was to cook." After three years and two children, Charollette's husband picked up and left. "I don't know if he rode off into the sunset or not," she says, " but he sure as hell rode off."

She stayed on at the ranch. The other cowhands adopted her and her daughters as members of their own family. "The cowboys here are settled, old-time hands," she says. "One has been here 20 years and another has been here for 15 years. They're nice guys, and they look after me and the girls. That's a real comfort."

Charollette and her daughters live in the mobile home cookhouse. They eat with the cowboys, who appreciate a little feminine company to break up the monotony of running cattle, haying, mending fences and living in a bunkhouse.

A Kitchen Queen

Burr hires single men mostly, so Charollette is viewed as sort of a queen, and, indeed she fits the role. She's a kitchen queen, albeit a bashful sovereign. "When I first came here, I was scared to death of the guys here," she says. She arrived at the height of haying season when some 30 men of every type were working. Some of that outfit were pretty unsavory, she recalls.

"Most of the crew came from an employment agency in Denver that sent out anyone they could sweep off the streets to fill their job quota. We had down-and-out bikers, winos, convicts and I don't know what all. I'm afraid of men anyway, and to be stuck out here with all those creeps was almost too much." The regular cowboys protected her, and gradually she got accustomed to the crews. She has had no trouble since then—well, almost no trouble.

"One time I cooked up a batch of ribs, and boy, they came out tough," Charollette says. "One of the older hands said he couldn't eat them. `Just chew harder,' I said. `But Missy,' he said, `I ain't got no teeth.'"

Teeth or not, the cowboys at the Burr try to help Charollette and ease her way in the kitchen.

"I get one day off a week and Fran (Bob's wife) fills in for me, but if I have to be gone, I leave food in the oven and the guys warm it up. They understand. In winter, the guys need big old ranch meals and I try to provide. I like them and they like me."

While life at the Burr Ranch is not all fun and games, it's not all that bad, either. Winters in the Park are long, and the ranch cuts back to five full-time cowboys. While the cold can be blistering, winter allows her peace and quiet that she enjoys.

"The boys use big work horse teams to feed the cattle. That's such a sight, and the deer, elk and moose wander down right into our yard. I love this place and I hate to even think about leaving."

Charollette planned to go to college and get an elementary education degree. She hoped to return to Walden to teach.

Her dream of coming back to the basin, devoting more time to her daughters and less to cooking for so many menfolk came true for Charollette. Since we visited the Burr Ranch, Charollette did indeed complete her degree with the Burrs' blessing. Currently back at the ranch, she's married to Dick Anderson, one of the top hands, and teaching school in Walden. Watching the men complete baling the tons of hay for winter to be sold and also used at the ranch, she notices the compacted haystacks resembling huge bread loaves. Charollette calls them doodles because they look like giant doodle bugs out in the fields.

When winter arrives, Charollette cooks good, basic ranch meals—meat, potatoes and other vegetables, and of course a great dessert with lots of hot coffee. Regardless of a cowboy's age, he's still a boy at heart, says Charollette, a boy with a mouth full of sweet teeth. She always has a dessert for her cowboys, even at breakfast.

Charollette Sanches' Cinnamon Rolls

1 package dry yeast

¾ cup scalded milk, cooled

¾ cup warm water

½ tablespoon salt

⅓ cup shortening

½ cup sugar

1 cup mashed potatoes

6 to 7 cups all-purpose flour

1 stick softened butter

cinnamon sugar (¾ cup sugar mixed with

2 teaspoons ground cinnamon)

Icing: 5 cups powdered sugar

1 tablespoon vanilla

Dissolve the yeast in ½ cup 70 degree water. Add the milk, ¾ cup water, salt, shortening, sugar, potatoes and 4 cups flour. Beat until smooth. Add enough flour until it's easy to handle. Knead 10 minutes or until smooth and elastic. Place in greased bowl and let rise until it has doubled.

Punch down and divide in half. Roll out a half into a rectangle. Spread the butter over the dough and sprinkle heavily with cinnamon sugar. Roll up and cut into 1" slices and place in greased baking pan and let rise for one hour. Repeat with second half.

Bake for approximately 20 minutes at 375 degrees F.

To make the icing, combine the sugar, vanilla and enough water to make it smooth. Top the hot rolls with the icing.

Yield: 2 dozen small or 12 large cinnamon rolls.

THE LYONS PLACE
CRAIG, COLORADO

RANCH NEAR THE END OF THE ROAD
Betty Lou "Sarge" Lyons, Woman of the West

About six miles south of Craig near the Moffat-Routt county lines, Colorado Highway 394 just runs out of blacktop, giving way to wide, open wheat fields interspersed with livestock pastures, rolling hills and small trout streams lined with willows; here deer, elk and moose hide in the breaks.

In 1978, this country drew Otis and Betty Lou Lyons, who already owned several ranches. Maybe their attraction for the property was in part created from the fact that the highway ended here, or perhaps the ranch seemed charming because the place had acquired a patina of age. The ranch house was built in 1895, with landscaping that includes ancient elms that probably go back a few hundred years. Betty Lou says a hedge on the ranch property dates back half a century.

In any case, the Lyons loved this place, and they soon bought the ranch. Otis, Betty Lou and their older sons run their family operation. Their youngest, who plans to marry soon, is in college and doing well riding on the rodeo circuit. The older sons, with their wives, help run the ranch. To the Lyons boys, even if they're grown, Betty Lou is still "Sarge."

"I wore out a belt on them when they were little," says Betty Lou. "My efforts must have made an impression on them, because they still remember the belt and the discipline to this day."

Betty Lou wears the name "Sarge" like a badge of honor. Through her taciturn demeanor and her personal history, she typifies the woman of the West, who complains little and who faces life's challenges without flinching, as if she were staring down a gale-force wind.

WILLIAM JEFFCOAT AND THE MEEKER MASSACRE

Born in Iowa, her parents farmed. Her mother, she says, worked the fields all day alongside the menfolk, leaving their daughters to do the domestic chores. "Us girls had to do the cleaning and cooking," Betty Lou says. Since she was seven years old, Betty Lou Lyons has been farming, ranching, and of course, cooking. "You had to be tough to make it in them days," she says.

Betty Lou tells how her grandfather, William Jeffcoat, a Cherokee from Oklahoma, homesteaded with her half-Indian grandmother, Bessie Clark, near Meeker, Colorado, some 47 miles south of Craig. "When he arrived, he was so broke he didn't even own a horse, so he had to walk the last 40 miles from Rifle to Meeker," Betty Lou recalls.

In October 1879, Grandpa Jeffcoat arrived in Meeker at a bad time. The White River Utes had just rebelled against government policies enforced on the reservation by Indian agent Nathan Meeker. Following United States policy, Meeker, for whom the town was named, wanted the tribes to give up hunting and take up farming. He moved agency headquarters to the middle of the Utes' sacred hunting grounds, plowed up their pastures and ordered the Indians to kill off their buffalo ponies. The Utes were enraged. Meeker, fearing for his life, ordered in the cavalry. On September 29, the Utes attacked the soldiers, killing 11 men and most of the soldiers' horses.

The siege raged on until October 5, when a rescue column arrived from Cheyenne, 280 miles to the north. Though the Indians had withdrawn by this time, they had killed Meeker and taken his wife and daughter hostage. William Jeffcoat had just arrived in the town of Meeker when the surviving Army scout rode in with news of the massacre, Betty Lou relates.

Her Cherokee heritage, her youth in Iowa and ranching in Colorado have given her an appreciation of different cultures and different ways of life, but farming and ranching have always meant the most to her. Raised in Georgia, her husband Otis is from farming stock too. He and Betty Lou married in Craig, Colorado in 1953. "Otis has farmed and ranched all his life, just like me," Betty Lou says. "We probably always will be farmers and ranchers."

One of her sons married a girl of Scottish descent, and with her penchant for various cultures, Betty Lou has been learning about the Scots, especially through their cooking. Scottish sheepherder's pie has become one of her favorite recipes. "I try to vary our meals," says Betty Lou. "I cook a lot of venison and elk, as well as beef and lamb."

The area near Craig abounds in game, and hunting is a popular activity. The family supplemented income by taking in up to 50 or 60 hunters a season, and Otis served as a guide for hunting parties. But now that Otis and Betty Lou are getting older, they don't run a hunting camp any more.

Photographer Charles Belden captured classic ranch scenes like this one in the early 1900's.

Range Wars, Woollies and Chariots

The open, rolling hills of Moffat County provide prime grazing turf for sheep. Betty Lou says that Grandpa Lyons once ran sheep on his homestead, as did many area ranchers.

In 1869, Colorado boasted more sheep than cattle, but that statistic didn't convince cattlemen to be any more receptive to woollies. Moffat County saw some bloody battles over sheep farming.

"This old house we live in is right in the center of the fight," says Betty Lou. "Our house was built of rough-cut logs, but since we have drywall inside, I haven't seen any bullet holes, but they used to do a lot of shooting hereabouts."

In 1874, as a matter of fact, angry ranchers killed 234 sheep belonging to a Jeremiah Booth, and in 1894, night riders ran more than 3,000 sheep off a cliff. This murderous activity the perpetrators called, "rimrocking." In 1894, yet another 1,500 sheep met the same fate, but the sheepherders persisted, and gradually cattlemen began to see the wool and mutton producers were not going to go away.

The Lyonses themselves once ran some sheep, but now that their sons have grown up, they have been able to cut back on their work schedule to a degree. Currently, Otis sells real estate in Craig, while keeping active tending his cattle, horses and providing hay for the stock. "We run commercial Angus," Betty Lou says. "We also raise American quarter horses. We like horses with lots of thoroughbred blood."

The Lyonses have owned show horses, cow horses, roping horses and now they have chariot horses. Otis loves to run them with his sons. The Lyonses also use their quarter horses not only to work cattle, but for chariot racing as well. The Lyons run their ponies in the Northwest Chariot circuit, and they do well at the meets. "We really enjoy chariot racing," Betty Lou says. "It's so exciting and it really makes the winters go by quickly."

Otis and Betty also continue their long-time involvement in rodeo. She once rode the local circuit as a barrel racer and Otis roped in jackpot rodeos. They started the Old Timer's Rodeo in Craig that takes place during the county fair. Otis serves as director, and Betty is treasurer.

"We're gung ho on rodeo," she says. They also run the Little Britches Rodeo which features events for youngsters under 18 years of age. Betty has also been superintendent of the Moffat County Fair cattle show, a food judge for 15 years, a 4-H leader for 20 years and state 4-H vice president for six years. Sarge also operates the hay baler in the summer when she's not in the kitchen, and enjoys riding out to check the cattle.

The Lyonses have had many a memorable time on horseback. Betty says that once she had a little black mare she rode out to cut cows in the 4-foot-high sagebrush. Her horse jumped right over some brush and threw Betty, but that didn't stop her mare. "That little bugger went and put the cow away and came back and got me. She was a real working little mare."

Betty also owned another mare they named Gee Whiz. She recalls that one year a hired hand rode Gee Whiz out to gather yearlings, but he forgot his bridle and so was riding her with just a halter.

"He couldn't turn her for nothing," Betty says. "She just ran where she wanted with the boy screaming at the top of his lungs, 'Whoa, you son-of-a-bitch, whoa!'"

Shovel and Shut Up!

That hand must have learned to swear from Sarge, who says she learned her cussing in the kitchen. "I've made some godawful messes," she says, "and it makes me mad every time I think about it." Just after she married she tried to bake bread for the first time and she forgot to add yeast. Out popped the bread from her oven, hard as a rock.

She buried her mistake out in the yard so Otis wouldn't discover her crime, but the dog dug up the evidence, gnawing on it awhile before he left it in the driveway. Otis says the dadburn bread was so hard, when he hit it with the tractor, on coming home, the bread nearly tipped him over. "I could've killed that damn dog," Betty says.

Somehow word of Betty's buried bread trick got out to her friend May, who had a bread mishap of her own. She too took her mistake out to bury it, but her problem was compounded by the fact that she had used too much yeast, and the dough rose so much that the bread was unmanageable.

May took her kitchen disaster up a hill behind her house and covered the bread with rocks. When the sun rose up and warmed the rocks, the dough expanded and started creeping down the hillside. May's husband came home from his fields at noon, when lo and behold he spied a strange mass of runaway stuff slip-sliding down the hill. "May," he asked his wife, "what the hell is that under those rocks up there?"

After those early trials and tribulations, disasters and desperations, Betty Lou Lyons has become a splendid cook. She loves her crockpot and prepares meal ingredients the night before, placing them in the pot the next morning and letting them simmer all day until the whole house is permeated with cooking aromas. When she and the family return from a hard day on horseback, or after haying or hunting, there's dinner all ready and waiting. "It took me a little while to learn how to cook," she says, "but now, after 50 years, I think I'm about to get the hang of it."

Betty says she has a D.E. degree in cooking. "That's Direct Experience. You name it and I've tried it." One recipe that's proved popular with her family over the years is her green chili. "You will enjoy it," she barks. Remember, any wish coming from Sarge is just like a command. So, when she says, "Eat," then everyone follows suit, and when she says "Enjoy!", then everyone pays attention and digs in with gusto.

Betty "Sarge" Lyons' Green Chili

2 pounds pork roast

6 cups water

1 4-ounce can chopped New Mexican green chiles.

dash of garlic salt or to taste.

1 clove garlic, chopped

½ cup chopped onion

1 16-ounce can stewed tomatoes

½ teaspoon dry oregano

½ cup cornstarch

salt and pepper to taste.

Simmer the roast in the water until done. Remove and cut the meat into small pieces.

Combine the meat, chiles, garlic salt, garlic clove, onion and tomatoes, then cook for 10 minutes. Add the oregano and simmer for 10 more minutes.

Mix cornstarch with water to make a smooth paste. Slowly add to the other ingredients to thicken. Salt and pepper to taste.

Serves: 4

Betty's green chili is great on eggs, hamburgers and tacos, or in burritos and omelettes...or simply by itself. When served alone, garnish to taste with longhorn cheese.

Lay Valley Ranch

CRAIG, COLORADO

WHERE THE BUFFALO STILL ROAM
Buffalo Broker Dan Martin, Owner-Operator and Head Cook

Between Craig and the Utah state line, Lay Valley opens onto high range country. In ancient prehistoric times, before humans arrived, Lay Valley was covered by an inland sea. Later, a huge swamp served as habitat for dinosaurs. Still later, great herds of American bison, commonly called buffalo, roamed throughout the valley.

This country is steeped in history. Davy Crockett supposedly passed through here in 1837, and intrepid explorer John Fremont traversed what is now Moffat county in 1844, guided by famous army scout Kit Carson.

About 17 miles west of Craig, along Highway 318, the Lay Valley Ranch differs markedly from most ranches in the West, and owner-operator Dan Martin seems to be cut from different cloth than most ranchers as well. On Martin's ranch the visitor won't see cattle, sheep or hogs. Dan raises buffalo. He also arranges buffalo hunts, and he's a complete buffalo broker, selling hides, heads and meat. From wholes, halves, and quarters right down to two pounds of buffalo burger, Dan Martin stands ready to sell hungry consumers any cut of bison meat they might desire.

BUFFALO TALES

How does a mild-mannered, soft-spoken, well-educated rancher get into the buffalo business? Dan Martin's adventure with buffalo began one Friday night at the local Craig watering hole. Ken McDowell, an old mountain man acquaintance, and Dan started talking about the Old West and how buffalo were a symbol of that bygone era.

"The buffalo was everything to the Plains Indians who lived around here," says Dan. "It provided them clothing, shelter and food."

The tavern talk ran long and loud, and pretty soon Dan found himself surrounded by rancher types who said that the passing of the buffalo wasn't such a bad thing at all.

"Buff'la were hard on ranges, water holes and fences," said one grizzled cowhand. "You can never domesticate 'em."

"Wait a minute," Dan argued. "Buffalo are just another animal, and how they act depends on how you treat them." That comment sparked the ranchers to challenge Dan to prove his point, and in the West, once you make a stand, you don't dare back down. "By golly," Dan grins, "I ended up having to buy two of the damn things."

So, Dan purchased two calves from another Colorado ranch. Then he bought three adults the next year from a Nebraska supplier. The calves had been no trouble, but when he turned loose those adults, they took off down the road.

Buffalo are fast. Dan clocked one at 50 miles an hour. There's no way to outrun one on foot and they can even beat a racehorse for a short distance. After a brief chase, Dan drove ahead of the escapees in his pickup, enticed them with grain and brought them back home. "They've been here ever since," Dan says.

Buffalo know what they want and they usually get it, too. Martin recalls one hand who thought he could master a female. "We had one old kid here who was gonna show us how to cut a cow out of the herd with his horse," Dan says. "That cow blasted out of the bunch and trampled right over the top of him, horse and all. "Cajoling, coaxing, and talking nice and easy—that's the way to work buffalo. Bison will not tolerate pushing and crowding the way cattle, sheep or horses will. "The best thing to do with buffalo," Dan says, "is to leave 'em alone." He neither brands, castrates, dehorns or doctors his bison. He feeds them, loves them and gives them lots of room. He pretty much stays away from his buffalo, especially cows at calving time. "No use to stir 'em up and get 'em on the fight," he says.

Buffalo start calving at three years and they produce offspring every year for over 30 years. Dan says they start out slow, but they have continuity.

Even though buffalo are generally quiet, sociable animals, they have their fights and family spats too. Dan likens them to children who are always quarreling. But if any intruder dares to approach, they drop their internal squabbling and gang up on the outsider.

"They'll go after a dog or a coyote. Buffalo stick together. When you take on one, you

Dan Martin on the Lay Valley Buffalo Ranch, Craig, CO.

have to fight the whole herd," Dan observes.

At the National Stock Show in Denver, held each winter, buffalo ranchers had to give up using ring attendants altogether, because they tried to crowd and force the buffalo. "People were getting hurt," Dan says. "Animals were crashing over gates, busting up equipment and running all over the place. They're not mean. They just take care of themselves and by God, they're big enough to do it."

Dan's $10,000 crowding chute stands neglected at his ranch. According to Dan, a buffalo actually handles and hauls easier than an Angus bull.

"They simply get in the trailer and lie down and they don't rile," he says. Dan's hauled and shipped lots of buffalo, some as far away as Florida, with few problems. "They're neat animals. They've got a little personality to them," he says.

A BULL MARKET IN BUFFALO

Dan believes there's a bull market in buffalo, and slowly more ranchers are starting to agree. Suppliers can't keep up with demand now. Financing to get into the buffalo business is comparatively easy, says Dan, because bankers want to get back buffalo ranchers.

Most cattle people can't handle buffalo, according to Dan. "They want to chase 'em with dogs and rope 'em with horses." Dan shakes his head. "You can't do that with buffalo. Once you get 'em mad, now by God, you got your hands full."

He says they eat about a third as much as cattle and they produce more meat than just about any commercial cattle.

"A buffalo is essentially a wild animal like an elk," Dan says, "while a Hereford is basically a meat machine, eating all the time. It takes a lot of goodies to keep that white baldy face going. And buffalo will eat a greater variety of plants than will cattle. They water just once a day and rest a lot." Despite what those ranchers told Dan way back before he started in the buffalo business, he insists bison are not near as hard on range as cattle are. Dan should know. He is no four-cow farmer. He's a range management specialist who worked for the Bureau of Land Management (BLM) in Oregon and Montana before moving to Colorado. Dan was born in Ohio, but he always wanted to come West, and the range management job let him do just that. He loves the high range around Craig.

Dan knows that buffalo meat will never replace beef, but he says buffalo causes no known allergic reactions and it's comparatively lean. Today's beef business reminds him of what's going on in the American automobile industry. "They're trying to sell big cars in a small car market just like cattle growers are still trying to sell fat steers in a lean meat market."

Dan ships all over the U.S., including New York and Hawaii, but his biggest market is still in Denver. The customer pays the freight and there's no middle-man for his U.S.D.A-inspected buffalo.

Only about 70,000 buffalo remain in the United States. Most are owned by small producers who run 10 or fewer animals. The largest herd (9,000) is in South Dakota. Cable TV producer Ted Turner has purchased an old, large Montana ranch and converted the property to the buffalo business.

"Don't overcook bison," Dan cautions would-be buffalo chefs. "The meat's finer fibers and lack of intermuscular fat transmits heat faster than beef. Most cooks tend to use high heat on bison meat and that's a mistake. Medium rare is preferable, and you don't have to slop a bunch of sauce or goop over the meat."

For any beef recipe there's a buffalo substitute that, in Dan's opinion, yields better results. He fancies using a wok and says that this method is quicker and easier than skillet or dutch oven cooking. The secret to wok-cooked bison is in the preparation. Once the meat hits the metal, a meal goes very fast. "You only need three woks to cook what you would using four or more skillets." He expressed surprise that more Americans haven't caught on to this easy-to-use cooking utensil developed in ancient China.

Dan says he first learned cooking skills as a Boy Scout. He became fascinated when one of his leaders prepared fry bread on a camping trip. He tried many times to make fry bread before he finally got the hang of it. He compares cooking to painting, music, or any fine art that requires total concentration. Dan tried out his early culinary experiments on his grandfather, who critiqued his efforts. "He ate Tums by the handful because he had a real bad stomach," Dan says. "He was gentle and helpful; for that I'll always be grateful."

To avoid killing off his grandfather, a determined Dan set off to the woods and tried his recipes on the wild critters.

"I bought 50 pounds of flour and went up to Rabbit Ears Pass, where I camped out and just made biscuits the whole time," Dan remembers. "Some of 'em were so bad even the jays and chipmunks wouldn't touch 'em. But, by golly, I learned to cook."

Dan takes great pride in his small ranch, and even though he wears so many hats, he keeps the house sparkling, the lawn trimmed, and is a fastidious chef. For him, cooking provides enjoyment and reward. He believes spices give meat life. "Centuries ago the Europeans risked their lives sailing around the world to search for spice. If it was worth it to them, it's worth it to me. I like spices and I use them, by golly."

The thrill of cooking, says Dan, is making a cut of meat into a delectable dish. Of course beef can be substituted for bison in his recipes, but it's just not the same as buffalo. "If you can't get bison locally," he adds, "just get in touch, and I'll be glad to help you out." For further information, contact Dan Martin, Lay Valley Bison Ranch, 19727 County Road 17, Craig, CO. 81625, Ph.:(303) 824-9207.

Dan Martin's
Buffalo-Broccoli Stir-Fry

⅓ cup soy sauce

2 tablespoons cider vinegar

¾ tablespoon sugar

1 beef bouillon cube

⅓ cup water

3 tablespoons cornstarch plus

2 teaspoons cornstarch

3 tablespoons peanut oil (won't burn)

2 large cloves garlic, crushed

1 pound buffalo steak, cut in ⅛" slices,

or substitute flank, etc. (flank, top, round or sirloin)

1 large onion, chopped

1½ cup broccoli florets

¼ pound fresh mushrooms, cut in ⅛" slices

Chinese noodles

Mix together the soy sauce, vinegar and sugar. In another container, mix the bouillon, water, and cornstarch. As with all stir-fry recipes, all cutting and chopping must be done in advance. Add 1½ teaspoons oil to a skillet or wok and heat over med-hi. Add the garlic to the wok. Add the meat and stir-fry for 2 minutes or until the meat is medium brown but pink in center. Remove the meat and drain the pan juices and save. Add 1 tablespoon of oil to the wok, and when hot, add the onion and broccoli. Stir-fry for 2 minutes or until crisp and tender. Add the remaining oil around the edge of skillet or wok, and add the broccoli, mushrooms, and onions. Stir-fry for an additional 2 minutes. Add the meat, pan juices, and soy sauce mixture.

Stir, cover, and cook for 2 minutes.

Stir cornstarch mixture and pour into skillet or wok. Cook, stirring constantly, for 2 or 3 minutes until thickened. Serve over Chinese noodles and savor.

Serves: 4 to 6

THREE SPRINGS RANCH
DINOSAUR, COLORADO

A TOUCH OF THE OLD LONGHORN DAYS
Judy Beard, Kitchen Rebel

Hidden away down in the southwest corner of Moffat County, the Three Springs ranch house nestles in a covey of huge elm trees a couple of miles off Highway 40 close to the Utah line. The house is surrounded by an animal-proof fence that also guards a large garden from marauding deer, horses, cattle and sheep.

North of the ranch is the Dinosaur National Monument. A sprawling preserve that displays ancient reptile remains, it follows the Yampa River drainage as it wanders into Utah, following the Green River to just north of the little town of Jensen. In this high plains country the grass is good, but sparse. Cattle must be hardy to survive and prosper here. But thanks to ranch manager Minford Beard and his wife Judy, the cattle and horses on the Three Springs do just fine.

In 1970, when the Beards took over, they found the more than 100,000 deeded and leased acres that make up the Three Springs were in bad condition.

"There wasn't a fence on the place that would hold a critter," Judy says. "The only way we could keep horses was to tie them up. We worked unmercifully hard during those first few years." Their toil soon began to pay off and they say the owners pretty much let them do as they see fit on the property.

The ranch once ran Herefords, but Minford and Judy have started to cross Texas longhorn bulls with their cows. They love their hardy longhorns, that are a legacy of the Old West. "Longhorn bulls bred to our first-calf heifers have eliminated the calf-pulling job we hate so bad," says Judy. "We like quiet cattle. We're raising market beef and we're pretty serious about it."

The Beards have found pure Herefords don't produce enough milk for their calves on this high desert range. Crossbreeding and raising replacement heifers produces a tough animal suited to this severe country. "Our cows get to know us and come to us if they have problems," Judy says. "We keep them friendly. That's why we don't use dogs here. We don't dislike dogs, but cows sure hate them."

At first Judy served as Minford's only ranch hand, but now a crew of three leaves Judy more home time, not that she loves domestic life. "When lunch goes out of here, it's apt to be sardines, crackers and fig newtons," she says. "I hate domestic stuff. I'm not a domestic person. I love my home and I love to bake, but I don't consider myself a cook. I bake bread and I make a mess and that don't make me a cook."

A REBEL AND A REAL JILLAROO

If Judy sounds like a kitchen rebel, that's because she is. Born July 5, 1941 on a dairy farm in Wheatland County, New York, she learned to milk like most kids learn to walk. When she was 10, her family sold the farm and moved to Malibu, California, a decision she disliked. From then on she plotted her escape, studying state maps, until she discovered Nevada had fewer people per square mile than any other state.

37

"By golly, that's where I wanted to be," says Judy. At age 18 she ran away to visit her friend Lillian Darrough near Round Mountain, Nevada, and she went to work for ranch manager Smokey Bowman near Tonopah. At first, she thought her parents might come to drag her back to Malibu, but they never showed.

Tonopah features some of the most open, desolate country in America. Cowboys say that Nevada is a good home for the old and a good school for the young, a perfect place for a young buckaroo, or jillaroo, as female buckaroos are called.

"The Bowman place was a real hair-and-shit operation," Judy says. She started learning about range cattle, seeing a squeeze chute for the first time, as well as branding, castrating, dehorning and doctoring.

She fell in love with ranch life and drew a hand's pay as a real cowgirl. "I thought I was in heaven," she says. "There were no people around, only cows and calves. Cows are wonderful friends. If I got lonesome, I'd just go visit with the cattle. They're peaceful and they're wonderful listeners."

Eventually Judy married Smokey but, to her consternation, she found he was a typical restless cowboy. He and Judy moved a lot over the next few years. "Smokey was fiddle-footed in the extreme," she says. His footloose ways took them to construction jobs all over the West, to ranches, and even to a logging job on Deep Creek, near White Sulphur Springs, Montana.

Judy worked as hard as any man and even put in a stint setting chokers on logs. The foreman couldn't believe it. Setting chokers is not women's work. It's hard and dangerous work, but Judy won't take no for an answer. She's spent her energies and time in a man's world and never had children.

In winter, when construction, logging and ranching slowed down, Judy and Smokey took odd jobs, or did some trapping, and Judy even did some cooking when she found work.

"Living with Smoke was never easy," she says, "but it was always interesting." Smokey taught her about taxidermy, camping, cooking, cattle and cowboying. She learned how to run a bulldozer on construction jobs, but often she was allowed just to grease and change oil on heavy construction equipment.

A Sure Enough Cowman

During one winter near Rangely, Colorado, south of Dinosaur, Judy hired on to feed cows for rancher Minford Beard. Minford ranched on White River between Rangely and Meeker then, and Judy saw he was a sure enough cowman.

Minford was born on the White River. "He never even got to town until he was 12," she recalls. "On his first trip to town he had a hell'va time 'cause he couldn't figure out where to go to the bathroom. He'd never seen indoor plumbing." Minford's 74 now (1991) and he's still a real top hand. He's good with cows and he can work on equipment when he has to, Judy says.

"I fell head over heels in lust with him and got shed of Smoke," she says. According to her, they were married December 27, 1968, but Minford still refuses to agree with her on the day and year when they tied the knot.

Minford also picked up income by packing and dude outfitting for fall hunting trips. Judy helped with the horses because she was such a Kitchen Calamity Jane, except for her bread baking. Each of them had a string of pack horses; Judy's were more experienced, Minford packed the colts. Save for blizzards, Judy enjoyed their pack trips. "Even the bad days were okay," she says.

In the spring of 1970 they sold their outfitting business and planned to head north to Yukon Territory, but they never made it. Instead they wandered around the country, visiting relatives and "riding the grubline," as she puts it.

While in Louisiana they visited some old hunting clients who had become fast friends and who had just bought the Three Springs Ranch. Their old hunting partners became their new investment partners when they asked the couple to take over the ranch.

Minford's grandfather had homesteaded the original Three Springs Ranch, and Minford's mother was raised right there. It was an offer he couldn't refuse.

In addition to raising longhorn-Hereford crosses, Judy and Minford are also crossing longhorns with Highlands, which they say produces excellent beef.

"The beef market's changing," Judy says. "People are swinging away from fatty beef. Longhorns fatten like elk. You get bulk without fat, and that's what today's consumer wants."

Judy's conscious of consumer trends for healthy food. She's become involved in knowing about the "subtle energies" of food and how these energies relate to agricultural prac-

tices. She's convinced she can discover through research how to omit toxic chemicals from agricultural practices. "I try to find non-toxic compounds that help in my gardening and in our ranching," she says.

Each year Judy puts in a large garden and raises chickens and turkeys. She still does a little taxidermy, but she says she doesn't do any for Minford, because he's too picky. They've hunted the world over and their living room is chock full of trophies. "Next to cattle, horses and me," Judy says, "hunting is Minford's first love."

When Judy's not riding for Minford, putting up hay, gardening, skinning coyotes or painting bull parts, she does find time in the kitchen. She's arranged everything for efficiency, so that she can get her cooking done and get on with more fun activities around her ranch. She tapes her favorite recipes to the

Judy Beard holding her hand-crafted walking sticks, Three Springs Ranch.

inside of her kitchen cabinets, so they are ready and available to read without having to dig them out and prop them up while she's involved mixing and preparing dishes.

In addition to all her other interests, Judy has come up with a very specialized business she calls Neatstuff. She buys butchered bull penises and makes walking sticks out of them. All shellacked and shiny, the renovated parts look great, and they fulfill their walking-stick function perfectly. What an unusual gift and what a conversation piece. They don't come cheap, though. But those bulls don't give up their parts easily, either.

For information about Judy, her Subtle Energies Program and her NEATSTUFF, contact her at 28507 Highway 40, Dinosaur, CO. 81610, Ph.: (303) 374-2327.

Judy Beard's Bread

1 cup honey
2 cups warm water
4 ounces granulated yeast
1 cup melted butter
2 tablespoons salt
2 eggs
1 cup powdered milk
4 cups whole wheat flour
4 cups unbleached flour

Dissolve the honey in the warm water. Scatter the yeast over the top and stir to dissolve. Set aside and allow to foam. Add the butter, salt, eggs, and milk. Mix these ingredients thoroughly with an electric mixer, if you have one. Add equal amounts of whole wheat and unbleached flour a few cups at a time, finally working with hands at the last of the flour Knead for 10 minutes or until smooth and elastic.

Cover and allow dough to double in size one time. Punch down; form into loaves and let rise in pans. Bake at 350 degrees F. for about 45 minutes.

Glaze bread fresh from the oven with butter so that loaves turn out nice and soft. Try slicing loaves, sacking, then freezing for later use. Frozen slices toast well and the bread will not spoil.

Yield: 3 5x9-inch loaves.

HISTORIC FORKS RANCH
SHERIDAN, WYOMING

CAKES, SNAKES, AND A FEW GOOD LAUGHS
Carol Myers, Comedian Cook

The Forks Ranch, part of the historic Kendrick Cattle Company, encompasses about 209,000 wind-sculpted acres along the Wyoming-Montana border. The Forks occupies the barren ridges, breaks and coulees of the Powder River drainage. A few scraggled cottonwoods perch along Hanging Woman Creek or other small tributaries and afford shelter against the winds.

Born in Cherokee County, Texas in 1857 and orphaned in his youth, John B. Kendrick assembled a Wyoming cattle empire, constructed a mansion in Sheridan, and became a political power in the early 1900s.

Kendrick's career began at age 15. He became foreman on the Wyoming spread owned by Texas rancher Charles Wulfgen after participating in a cattle drive in the cowboy state during 1879.

Kendrick purchased the OW Ranch and moved there in 1891, after he married Wulfgen's daughter Eula. Kendrick prospered and added more properties to the OW. In 1908, he began building Trail's End, his 18-room mansion that would take five years and $165,000 to complete. Replete with eight baths, eight porches, an elevator and central vacuum cleaning system, the coal-heated Trail's End was Kendrick's monument to his political and social prominence.

In 1911, he ran unsuccessfully for the Senate, but the following year was elected Wyoming governor. Five years later, while still governor, Kendrick won the senatorial seat he coveted, serving two additional terms in that office until, in 1933, he died at age 76. Eula Kendricks continued living at Trail's End until 1961, when she, too, passed away.

In 1963, the Sheridan County Historical Society managed and ran the property as a museum. In 1983 they assumed ownership of Trail's End.

A SELF-PROCLAIMED HILLMAN, POET AND FARMER

It's a long and dusty drive out of Sheridan to the Forks. The town closest to the ranch is Decker, Montana, little more than a trading post where miners from Peabody Coal Company cash their paychecks, drive trucks the size of battleships, and wield coal shovels as big as Sherman tanks that terrify the locals.

Out in the Wyoming chaparral the Forks provides a home to three cowboys, three

41

ranch hands and a mechanic named Hap Myers, who married the ranch cook, Carol Parker Myers. Born on a dryland farm south of Decker, Wyoming, Carol started cooking at the Forks in 1970, after graduating from high school as one of only two students who attended the one-room school in Pine Butte. Carol says she had been bucked off a horse and was recovering from two broken vertebrae when ranch manager Walter "Spud" Murphy asked her to fill in as cook out at the Forks.

Carol's father, E.L. "Tod" Parker, a self-proclaimed hillman, poet and farmer, scratched out a living on the dry ridges of the open Wyoming plains far from Sheridan, where Carol's two older sisters and mother had moved to escape the isolation of the family farm. At an early age Carol became her father's hand, cowboy, chore girl and cook.

Carol's father expounded on farming, family life, taxes, and the weather, but his favorite subject was the Rural Electric Association (REA). He scrawled his observations on the back of seed tags, cigarette wrappers and toilet paper, stuffing these scraps in all his pockets. She encouraged him to send his poem, "Letter to the REA," to the REA monthly. They published the work. Encouraged, Tod Parker sent in many more poems which also saw print.

Tod created his own poetry anthology which he published, titled Thoughts of a Hillman. The little book pleads with the REA to get power to his place and offers praise to the association in poems such as "Meter Nerves," "Outages," "Overdue Bill" and "Ode to a Meter on a Rural Schoolhouse." He also praised Carol in his verse, and he gave her a legacy of hill country humor that she enjoys to this day. Tod Parker died recently of a heart attack, but Carol preserves his memory.

"I'm something of a prankster," she says, "so you'd better watch out for worms in your salad." Carol learned to laugh at life from her dad, who taught her that negative situations are just part of life.

"I remember the first time I tried to bake a cake," she says, recalling an incident that happened when she was in the first grade,

"The cake was so tough Dad couldn't eat it, so he just strapped it on his head and wore it for a hat."

AN UNINVITED GUEST

When she first arrived at the Forks, she learned her first recipes from a peg-legged cook who helped her get started. She beamed with pride when the old salt told her she was the first woman he had met who could "cook a 'tater without burning it."

Carol picked up her kitchen skills quickly that first year when she had to cook for twenty hands. Without a cookbook, she cut recipes from bread wrappers and cookie boxes, until later her mother gave her a recipe book.

An elongated log structure houses the bunkhouse, cookhouse and cook's apartment, with several guest cabins nearby. The buildings occupy a position at the base of a ridge that serves as a windbreak in winter. In summer the same pile of rocks provides a perfect place for rattlesnakes to sun themselves.

Once, in the midst of meal preparation, Carol watched in horror as a fat rattler rolled downhill, headed straight for her screen door. Fortunately, the door blocked the snake from becoming an uninvited kitchen guest. Carol's a stickler for cleanliness.

"I demand respect," she says. "No hats and no spurs. By God, you don't need spurs to ride a bench. I make the crews stack and clean their plates. The young guys think they don't have to mind. But, by God, I make 'em wash up and clean their boots and I make 'em say `please,' and `thank you, ma'am.'"

One young cowboy learned the error of his ways when he entered Carol's domain with muddy boots. She soon had him dancing with a mop, while the rest of the crew took heed of the punishment she had meted out.

During one weaning and shipping season a blizzard stranded the Forks. The bunkhouse leads directly to her dining area. She set up a chow line, so the 35 hands simply helped themselves and returned to their living area. This system worked so well, she adapted her methods for everyday use.

As mealtime approaches, Carol speeds up, until she resembles a video on fast forward. She flings pans and plates from cabinets as she mixes tea, lemonade and fruit juice, and sets out her main dish and dessert. She's right on time, and she wipes the sweat from her forehead, grinning as she pulls the dinner bell cord over the sink. In comes the crew, without hats and spurs, hands and faces washed, already loading plates. A few of the boys even shuffle around in their stocking feet to protect Carol's floor.

"This may look like a burnt offering to you," she quips, "but it's all you're gonna get out of this girl today."

Forks Chocolate Cake

½ cup shortening

1½ cups sugar

2 eggs

1 tablespoon vanilla

2 cups flour

⅓ cup cocoa

1 tablespoon soda

½ tablespoon salt

½ cup water

then add:

1 cup boiling, strong coffee.

Cream the shortening and sugar together. Add the eggs and vanilla and beat well. Sift together the flour, cocoa, soda, and salt. Add the dry ingredients alternately with the water. Add the coffee and beat to make a thin batter.

Pour in a greased and floured 13" x 9" cake pan. Bake at 325 degrees F. until it's done by the toothpick test. Takes about 45 minutes to bake.

Try either topping for a sweet treat.

French Silk Frosting

2 ounces melted unsweetened chocolate

⅔ cup soft butter

2⅔ cups powdered sugar

¾ tablespoon vanilla

2 tablespoons milk

Blend together the chocolate and butter. Then add the powdered sugar and vanilla.

Blend in a mixing bowl and gradually add the milk. Beat 'til smooth and fluffy.
Makes enough for a 13" x 9" cake.

Mocha Topping

1 cup sugar
¼ cup cornstarch
¼ tablespoon salt
2 cups cold strong coffee
unsweetened chocolate
2 tablespoons butter
1 tablespoon plus 1 teaspoon vanilla
2 cups of Dream Whip, whipped cream, or
2 packs Dream Whip

Mix together the sugar, cornstarch, and salt in a saucepan. Gradually stir in the coffee. Add the chocolate and cook, stirring constantly, until the mixture boils and thickens. Boil and stir for 1 minute and remove from heat.

Blend in the butter and vanilla. Press plastic wrap onto top and cool thoroughly. Fold the coffee mixture into the whipped cream, Cool Whip or Dream Whip.

Makes 5 cups, enough for a 13" x 9" cake.

To avoid making cake soggy, apply topping to individual servings.

Margaret Allamand brands one while Buck and the boys hold him down on the Staple 3 Ranch (see next page).

STAPLE 3 RANCH
MIDWEST, WYOMING

SHEEP RANCHING NEAR THUNDER BASIN
Margaret Allemand, International Cook

The town of Midwest, Wyoming is situated on I-25, about 50 miles north of Casper. Here, former Crow Indian country spreads in an open buffalo plain to the horizon. In the 1850s some bloody range wars took place near town, and during the Harding administration the infamous Teapot Dome scandal broke in the oil patch close to Midwest, when money-grubbing oil barons and a crooked politician named Albert Fall left their mark on national and Wyoming politics; a mark that still scars Wyoming political life.

About eight miles southeast of Midwest, down a dirt road that passes through a Navy oil reserve field, the Staple 3 Ranch operates under the capable management of Buck and Margaret Allemand, their daughter Mary and her husband Bill Owens, and the Allemands' three sons.

"We don't get many guests out here," Buck says. Security guards, gates, fences and surveillance cameras at the government oil field deter the casual visitor from approaching the Staple 3. Even a sprinkle of rain turns the access road into a quagmire of gumbo mud that would bog a killdeer.

The vast Salt Creek area, constant winds, isolation and dirt roads don't bother the Allemands one bit. They love the privacy and the peace of the open plains. The wind is their constant companion, drying roads and blowing snow from ridges in winter, allowing livestock to graze all year without being fed hay.

The Allemands own their own airplane, hangar and landing strip, so they can check water gaps in fence lines after summer storms and check their many pastures, or hunt coyotes that stalk sheep, calves and wildlife.

Buck's grandfather was a sheepherder, and came from France to America in 1880. The open Wyoming range with its short, heavy grass seemed an ideal place to run sheep, and in 1923 he purchased the Staple 3, where Buck was born in 1931. His father was born about 70 miles north of Midwest, in Buffalo, located in the heart of Johnson County. In the late 1800s range wars broke out in Wyoming. The Johnson County War began in 1892, when cattlemen hired outside guns to cut down marauding rustlers.

Fighting escalated, and the ranchers hired former Pinkerton agent Tom Horn, who in his new role as range detective advertised, "Killing is my specialty. I look upon it as a business proposition and I think I have a corner on the market." The fracas got out of hand when the range detective murdered a teen-age boy. Tom Horn was hanged by militia who had been called in to restore order to the county. The more recent past has been just as colorful in this part of Wyoming.

In the summer during the halcyon years at the Staple 3, herders from the world over moved more than 12,000 sheep with horses and dogs. In winter, the sheep roamed barren ridges where the animals preferred to graze. Herders from the Basque region of Spain, from Ireland, France, Mexico and Scotland formed an odd and taciturn bunch that preferred solitude, and occupied themselves keeping away coyotes. Some were poets and painters.

As the years went by, coyotes proliferated until, during the Allemands' final season sheep ranching, predators took 20 percent of their lambs. The Staple 3 now runs cattle, and the Allemands' children take a more active role in ranch affairs.

THE WIND IS THEIR COMPANION

An abundance of antelope range over the Staple 3. Buck and Margaret call them goats, because they lie around as tame as sheep. Other game, including mule deer, elk and a few bighorn sheep, rove the ranchlands. The Allemands' spacious, new two-story brick home features a den, the walls of which are covered with hunting trophies representing almost every North American game animal.

Like many ranchers, Buck and Margaret have supported the ranch by leading hunting parties over the years. In 1956, when the resourceful Allemands were married, they drove 37 horses for five days across country to the Pitchfork Ranch west of Meeteetse. At night, Buck crowded the horses into a corner on a fence line that served him as a corral.

"When I got to Meeteetse, I ran into an old kid named Jerk Steiner," Buck relates. "He looked like he'd been out in the weather all his life. He had a pickup and he helped me get a load of hay to those horses that were just about as starved as I was." Jerk Steiner worked at the Staple 3 as a saddlemaker, electrician, plumber, carpenter and jack-of-all-trades handyman. He built the Allemands' new ranch home.

Buck also tells how in 1969 he made $100 a day running one of the last cattle drives up old stock trails over Big Horn Mountain. Area newspapers covered the story. Buck's not the only one with a reputation, though.

Margaret's kitchen expertise has made her famous in these parts. Her contact over the years with herders from different lands has led Margaret to become a gourmet chef.

"I can cook in five different languages," she grins. "My mother was French. Her recipes please most folks."

A large picture window extends from the living room to the dining room and kitchen as well. The constant summer breezes ring the wind chimes outside her window and remind her that this is open country. From her modern kitchen, Margaret looks to the sheep sheds and cattle pens, the horse pasture, hangars and runway, and far to the east toward the rolling hills of Thunder Basin National Grasslands, a monument to native grasslands, home of buffalo, antelope and Indians that lived here long before the white man arrived.

LITTLE FOR BIG BUT HELL FOR STOUT

The Allemands are slowly letting the reins of the Staple 3 go to their eldest daughter Mary and her husband Bill, who was raised on a cattle ranch near Red Lodge, Montana. Bill worked his way through college as a government mule packer in Yellowstone. Mary's one of those small, wiry, tough people that cowboys say are "little for big but hell for stout." They met at the Allemands' K-Z Hunting Camp in Shoshone National Forest outside Yellowstone.

After they married, they worked as hands on a ranch west of Cody, Wyoming. They summered on Jim Mountain up the north fork of the Shoshone River, where they ran cattle, cooked out and tried to keep the grizzly bears out of their cabin and away from their cat, Black Jack. They cut holes in a plastic bucket where the terrified Black Jack could hide from bears as he rode in a salt pannier lashed to a mule's back. The feline even slept in the outhouse rafters, so great was his fear of bears.

"I reckon he thought he was safe up there," says Mary.

Late one afternoon, when Bill and Mary had returned from checking their cattle, they discovered Black Jack was missing. They searched for days, but still no Black Jack. Finally they ran into a rancher down in the valley who said he had seen a stray cat at his place. Bill and Mary went out there. When Black Jack spied Bill, he leaped up in his arms and rode all the way back to their cabin clinging to him.

Black Jack was not alone in his fear of bears. The bears also caused no end of grief to hikers and fishermen in the area.

"One day," says Mary, "we heard this awful noise and we just knew a bear was killing someone. We ran outside and heard this pitiful screaming, `Save me, save me.'" When they looked up the trail, Bill and Mary saw a backpacker running for his life and in hot pursuit, not a bear, but one of the Owens' mules. "The mule thought that backpack was a grain bag, and he was just trying to get a handout," Mary says, laughing and shaking her head.

The weather also caused some havoc up on Jim Mountain. Lightning storms in the back country can be fierce. One bolt struck a cow and killed her.

"Just knocked her to her knees," Mary says, " like she was praying, her tail sticking straight out. She stayed that way for three days before a bear came along and tipped her over."

Nowadays Bill and Mary are running registered Salier cattle at the Staple 3, producing a leaner beef more favored in today's beef market. The old sheep days are all but gone.

Bill and Mary learned vet skills from Mary's uncle, who lives in Three Forks. Being a long way from town, this knowledge has come in handy. Bill estimates he's performed some 80 C-sections on his cows. Mary helps with the doctoring and with embryo transplants.

She also takes pleasure in training her border collie, Tar, in a round corral, as he learns to circle on command, taking proper leads the same way a colt in training will. In horse training as well as in cooking, Mary defers to Bill, because she says he is good at both. Bill accuses her of sandbagging.

"She can ride the hair off a horse and she can cook as good as anyone," says Bill.

Grandmother Mary Immel's Applesauce Cake

½ cup shortening

1 cup sugar

1 egg, beaten

4 tablespoons hot water

2½ cups sifted flour

1½ cups applesauce

1 tablespoon baking soda

½ tablespoon ground cloves

¼ tablespoon ground nutmeg

1 cup raisins

½ cup walnuts

½ tablespoon salt

Mix all of the above into a batter and pour into a greased 8" x 11" pan.
Bake at 350 degrees F. for about 30 minutes or until done.

THE PITCHFORK
MEETEETSE, WYOMING

RIDING THE PITCHFORK
Shiela Whitlock, Trial and Error Cook

In 1866 a small, stocky nobleman named Count Otto von Liechtenstein left Germany and immigrated to New York, where for the next 11 years he participated in a banana import business with his two brothers. Like many frontiersmen, Otto Franc, or so he called himself, moved west because of failing health.

In 1878 he settled on the Greybull River, west of present-day Meeteetse, where he built a cabin and started buying cattle for the new ranch he was intending to start. He selected a pitchfork symbol as his brand and fought off the Shoshone and Mountain Crow who claimed his lands as their hunting grounds. As fast as he built his jackleg fences, the buffalo tore them down. As time went by, the Indians were confined to reservations, the buffalo were slaughtered, and the Pitchfork prospered.

In 1903, at age 57, Franc died in a hunting accident, leaving the ranch to his two sisters in Weisbaden, Germany. The two sold the Pitchfork to a wealthy banker from Great Falls, Montana named Louis Graham Phelps, who had moved to Chicago and founded the Continental Casualty Company. Phelps continued to add lands to the Pitchfork until in 1922, when he died, he owned about 250,000 acres and 40,000 cattle.

Phelps also built a three-story lodge on the ranch that is now listed in the National Register of Historic Places. Much of his memorabilia remains in the house today.

Phelps' daughter Frances married Charles Belden, whose many photographs documenting ranch life in the early 1900s have gained notoriety.

Born in San Francisco, Belden graduated from the Massachusetts Institute of Technology in 1910. His grandfather had been a member of the Donner party that had been stranded in the Sierras between Nevada and California during the winter of 1846. The group had resorted to cannibalism to survive.

Following graduation, Belden visited his former classmate Eugene Phelps at the Pitchfork, and fell in love with Phelps' sister Frances. In 1922, management of the Pitchfork passed to Charles and Eugene, although Belden preferred pursuing photography to running a ranch.

He spent many hours taking pictures of wild animals he came to know and respect, and the cowboy life he loved. Many of Belden's photographs, in addition to showing scenes from bunkhouse life, portray campfire cooking at the cowcamps. Belden's photographs were published in dailies all over the country. National Geographic also used his work. His shots were considered so definitive that Time-Life chose his pictures to illustrate cowboy life in its books on the American West. His darkroom remains in the attic of the ranch house, just as he left it.

In 1966, Belden left the Pitchfork. Tragically, he died of a self-inflicted gunshot wound in a motel room in St. Petersburg, Florida.

ONE OF THE LAST BEST PLACES ON EARTH

One of Belden's three daughters, Annice Belden Sommers, remains at the Pitchfork today as bookkeeper. Her daughter, Frances "Lili," married Jack Turnell, current ranch co-owner/manager, and co-author of *Brand of a Legend*, a history of the Pitchfork, written with Wyoming historian Bob Edgar, who owns the Trail Town Museum in Cody. The book is a treasury of those days of horses and cowboys, ranchers and Indians, of buffalo and bears, cold wet winters and hot dry summers—all the things that make the West what it was then and what it is now—one of the last best places on earth.

Jack Turnell continues in the tradition established by Belden. In the early 1980s, Turnell began efforts to preserve the last remaining colony of endangered black-footed ferrets that lived on the Pitchfork. Government studies of the colony showed ferrets were dying mysteriously. Biologists have trapped the remaining animals and are engaging in a captive breeding program to ensure their survival by returning them to their habitat on the ranch. Turnell recently received the Chevron National Conservation Award for his efforts to save the ferrets and his concerns about wildlife preservation.

Twenty-nine-year-old Sheila Whitlock cooks at the Pitchfork. Mother of two, she is married to Scott, a hand on the Z-T division of the sprawling Pitchfork. Scott represents the new breed of cowboy who can ride a horse, throw a rope, operate and repair machinery and do some spot welding when he has to. Ranches prize all-around hands. The day of the single-skill cowboy is gone, especially at the Pitchfork, which owns 1,600 mother cows and about a hundred brood mares. A new crop of colts is broken every year in preparation for the annual production sale held each October at the ranch, and a few colts are also sold at private treaty. The ranch welcomes visitors who want to look over the crop.

Molly Finch pushes on out the gate & John brings up the rear, Pitchfork Ranch.

Far from the old-time cookies who followed the boys out to cowcamps in their chuck wagons, Sheila prefers her kitchen and doesn't even like horses, even though she was raised on a ranch. From her kitchen window she watches deer, elk and moose wander into her yard.

"We have raccoons in the garbage cans and mountain lions in the colt pasture," she says.

To keep cougars from the colts, every night John, a hand who deals with the horses, sets up a propane-fired cannon that blasts intermittently. Called a Zon Gun, this device is supposed to spook the cats and drive them away. Several colts fell prey to the killer cats that kept the mares in a constant state of fear.

"This thing works well, and we haven't lost a colt since we started using it," John says. "It's kind of trial and error—the cats trying and our errors."

According to Sheila, her cooking is also the result of trial and error kitchen methods. She believes that careful experimentation with basic recipes leads the cook to new and great discoveries. She prepares meals for up to 80 hands during branding and roundup season, cowboys and cowgirls who line up to sample her dishes.

"I just stick with basics from the good old American West," says Sheila, "and I always have a dessert. Cowboys are big on dessert, don't you know."

Belden family recipes also play a part in life at the Pitchfork. Frances Phelps Belden, called Nana by family members, loved her favorite breakfast of creamed kidneys on toast. Lil Turnell, granddaughter of the great lady, says that while other members of the family are not as enthusiastic about the Belden breakfast, she and her brother don't consider morning complete without Nana's special treat.

Nana Belden's Breakfast
(Creamed Kidneys on Toast)

1 package kidneys
1 to 1½ cups white sauce
White Sauce:
2 tablespoons margarine
2 tablespoons flour
1 teaspoon salt
1½ cups milk

Melt margarine and stir in flour. Sauté for a couple of minutes to cook the flour. Add the salt. Slowly stir in the milk and whisk until the flour has dissolved in the milk. Simmer the sauce for 5 to 10 minutes, stirring constantly until the sauce thickens.

Yield: 1 to 1½ cups

Select small kidneys, as they will be more tender. Trim the fat and cut the kidneys into small, bite-sized pieces. Place them in a saucepan and cover with cold water. Bring just to boiling, but do not allow kidneys to remain in boiling water. Drain and rinse with cold water. Repeat this process two to three times until kidneys are cooked. Avoid bringing kidneys to boil more than four times, or they will be tough. There should be just a little pink left in the meat, which will cook out in the sauce.

Add the kidneys to the white sauce and heat. Don't allow sauce to boil, or it will toughen the kidneys. Serve over toast.

SQUAW CREEK RANCH
BIG HOLE, MONTANA

A FINE PLEACE FOR MEN AND CATTLE
Sheila Kirkpatrick, Cowgirl, Haberdasher and Cook

As the first red streaks of dawn appear over the Pioneer Mountains east of the Squaw Creek Ranch, 75-year-old ranch owner Wallace Christiansen mounts up and rides out. He never looks back to see if the crew is ready or not; the sun's coming up, and we're burning daylight.

While visiting the Squaw Creek to conduct interviews for this book, we've been invited to accompany the crew for fall roundup. It's mid-October, and Wally Christiansen has warned us to be ready to ride at first light. It's about 15 degrees below zero as we saddle in the dark. Ranch cook Sheila Kirkpatrick has prepared a monster breakfast of sausage and eggs, pancakes, hashbrowns and gravy. Now she quickly changes into her riding gear.

Horses snort and jump, frisking across the frost-covered meadow before settling down for a long ride to the top of the ridges. Rein chains jangle and spurs ring softly, as hoofbeats startle moose feeding in the willows behind the barn.

Every rider is silent, shoulders hunched against the cold, collar turned up high. On every head rests a hat custom-made by Sheila, who not only cooks, but has earned quite a reputation as hat designer and cowgirl. The hats have special earflaps that all the wranglers have turned down against the cold.

GET TOUGH, OR GET OUT

While romanticized in print and film, cowboying is a rough way of life. Cowboys and cowgirls are known for toughness and determination because of the demands made on them by ranching.

Up in the 6,200-foot-high Big Hole Valley in southwestern Montana, cowboying is as rough as it gets. The people, like the critters in the Big Hole, either get tough or they get out.

"The Big Hole," say local cowboys, "is a fine place for men and cattle, but it's damn tough on women and horses." These kinds of remarks make no impression on Sheila, wife of Buzz Kirkpatrick, Squaw Creek ranch manager, who met his wife-to-be when they both lived in Billings (pop. 70,000), Montana's largest city, where they both were raised. Now they call the Big Hole home.

From her kitchen window Sheila views the Big Hole River and in the distance, about 20 miles away, 9,210-foot Alder Peak marks not only the Continental Divide that separates the nation's watershed into east and west, but the demarcation of the Big Hole Valley from the Anaconda-Pintlar Wilderness.

The ranch features some of the finest fishing in the world. The Big Hole River is home to the exotic arctic grayling, relative of the trout, with a distinctive large dorsal fin. The river runs right through the ranch.

Montana Highway 43 separates the holding pens from the main house. Like many ranch houses built in the Big Hole, the house was constructed near the road to offer easy access to transportation. Winters here are so tough that the headquarters were located right near the old stage line over Mill Hill to Anaconda and Butte. The stage stopped here to rest the horses before making the last ten miles to overnight lodgings in Ralston, before proceeding over Mill Hill to Anaconda and finally Butte.

Within 20 feet of the highway following the old stage line, the large old log barn and elongated bunkhouse nest close by. Near the river and across the road there's a set of lodgepole corrals and pens, a squeeze chute and a scale house—as fine a family ranch as you will find.

Wallace Christiansen is the quintessential Montana rancher, tall as a ponderosa and straight as a lodgepole. He knows horses and cattle as well as anyone in the West and shows a fierce independence that marks that breed of men and women who have little time or patience with the prying questions of inquisitive writers and fumbling photographers who are curious about life in the Big Hole.

With his wife Ann, Christiansen owns not only the Squaw Creek spread, but another ranch that bears his name located near Wisdom, where he headquarters. He runs about 1,200 commercial Herefords and Black Baldie crosses he turns out in lower pasturage near the Anaconda-Pintlar Wilderness. Winter comes early and stays late in the "Land of the Big Snows," as the Indians called the Valley.

SHEILA'S FAMOUS HATS

As Sheila Kirkpatrick recalls, when she first joined Buzz in the Valley, she remembered all the stories she had heard during her childhood about Big Hole winters.

She was ready to pack up and head back to Billings after she attended a school orientation where administrators advised the parents to have in-town housing available for the kids, in case they were snowed in during a storm. Staff advised parents to have ground guides walk in front of their cars in order to see the roads.

"Buzz told me," Sheila says, "if you live here six months, you'll never want to leave. I couldn't believe the beauty of this place could ever overcome the harshness of the seasons, but it's true; I never want to leave the Valley."

People hereabouts also look forward to winter, when they can relax, work on hobbies indoors, ski, snowmobile, or hunt and trap varmints. Most of the men paint, do wood or leather work, and many women quilt or knit.

Her famous hats occupy Sheila. Her bunkhouse hat shop has purveyed custom chapeaus to country-western singer Hank Williams Jr., who has a ranch in the Big Hole, *Today Show* weatherman Willard Scott, actress Cheryl Ladd and George Bush. For Montana's centennial in 1989, the state commissioned her to create a limited edition of 500 official numbered Centennial hats.

When temperatures dip below zero, as they often do in the Big Hole, Sheila's most popular hat, the Big Hole Special with earflaps, can be seen on the heads of many a Valley cowboy and cowgirl. Many people say clothes make the man; for Sheila, hats make the man.

"I've always been interested in hats," she says. "You can tell a lot about people by the hats they wear and the way they wear them."

Sheila grew up around cowboys, cowgirls and ranchers, and saw lots of hats as a child. Her father announced rodeos and sometimes called auctions in Billings, where her truck-driver brother is also a part-time rodeo announcer.

After high school she married, had a child, divorced, and as a single parent, found a job in a Western-wear store where she cleaned and shaped hats for her cowboy and cowgirl customers. The more she knew about hats, the more she wanted to use her ideas to actually make one.

She took a job at an old, established hattery called Rands in Billings. She cleaned old hats, but her boss told her that she lacked the strength to pull new hats down over the shaping blocks.

"The word 'can't' is not in my vocabulary," Sheila says. "I don't know the meaning of the word."

Sheila's hat career was interrupted, however, when she quit Rands and hired on with an oil field crew digging ditches. When the oil boom went bust, she returned to Billings and got a job pen riding in a stockyard, where she met another pen rider, her husband-to-be, Buzz Kirkpatrick.

BIG RANCHER IN A SMALL WAY

After moving to the Big Hole with her daughter and Buzz's three sons, the couple had another girl. The older Kirkpatrick kids participate in high school rodeo. Cowboying seems to be in their blood. Buzz never brags about his own cowboy prowess, but Sheila gives him the praise he rightly deserves.

"I never look down when I'm chasing a critter," Buzz says. "That would scare me to death. I figure it's the horse's job to look where he's going. I just take care of business from the saddle horn up. Anything below that is the responsibility of the horse."

Gopher tunnels, badger burrows and bog holes are a constant hazard for riders in the Valley. A few years ago a horse fell over and rolled on Buzz, causing the saddle horn to mutilate his roping hand. Buzz's hand never healed completely, even after several operations. But he continues to cowboy because he loves his work, despite his tender hand.

When he has time, Buzz assists Sheila in the hat shop. He helps wash and clean old hats brought in for restoration. Ann Christiansen also lends a hand when she can. As Kirkpatrick's Custom Hattery has grown, Sheila has hired more help. Now Sheila is fulfilling her dream of becoming a custom hat designer.

"A hat should complement a person's natural skin tones," Sheila says. "And the hat should not overpower the appearance. There's more to buying a hat than just picking one off the shelf and setting it on your head."

Wally Christiansen is retiring now and turning his ranch over to his son in Dillon. Since our interview, the Christiansens have retired, and Sheila has moved her hatmaking, cleaning and blocking enterprise to a location near Highway 278 on the east side of Wisdom, a 20-mile commute for her, but she's serious about her hat business.

Buzz and Sheila have leased a ranch across the river, up the highway and out in the flat flood plains of the Big Hole.

"We're big ranchers in a small way," Sheila says. They've gathered up a few cows and have started their own herd. Buzz supplements the ranch income by packing for the Forest Service and clearing trails during the summer. When not making hats, Sheila is usually out riding with Buzz.

"You can't miss our place," Buzz says. "Just take the North Fork road, come up to the first set of corrals and turn right."

Sheila's Sloppy Joe
Bubble Burgers

1 pound hamburger meat
1 cup barbecue sauce
¼ cup chopped green peppers
¼ cup chopped onions
4 hamburger buns
4 slices cheddar cheese

Brown hamburger and drain off the grease. Add barbecue sauce, green peppers, and onions.

Cover and cook for 15 minutes.

Spoon the meat onto one half of a hamburger bun. Top with the cheese and broil until the cheese melts and bubbles.

Serves: 4

SAGE CREEK RANCH
DELL, MONTANA

LIVING HISTORY AT SAGE CREEK RANCH
Becky Mills, Live Turkey Cook

In the southwest corner of Montana, a few miles before the traveler crosses into Idaho on I-15 near Monida Pass, the little town of Dell (population 23) strings out along the road. Dell features the usual grocery store, gas pumps, hotel and bar, but the biggest attraction is Yesterday's Calf-A.

Formerly the town's one-room school, Yesterday's Calf-A has been converted into one of the finest eating places in the West. The food has that good, home-cooked flavor, with prices right out of the fifties. Savvy tourists, truckers, cowboys, cowgirls and ranchers come here to eat and to visit with the feisty owners, Ken and Ruth Berthelson. Other than Yesterday's Calf-A, the post office, the hotel and bar, there ain't a hell'va lot to the little ranching community of Dell.

During the long winters in this mile-high country, locals say the wind never blows—under 50 miles per hour. Residents expect snow during any month of the year.

To some, this place might seem like a little hell, but the southwest corner of Beaverhead County is actually a little paradise. Superb territory for livestock, the high country traps lots of snow in winter and spring, and the native grass flourishes on rolling, open ridges which swoop down from the Tendoy Mountains to the west, and the Continental Divide to the south.

About eight miles north of Dell up a winding country road, the Cooke Sheep Company once ran over 25,000 woollies on the largest sheep ranch in Beaverhead County. Now owned by the Matador Cattle Company, the Sage Creek, as the ranch is called now, runs Hereford cows.

According to John Lincoln in his book *Rich Grass and Sweet Water: Ranch Life With the Koch Matador Cattle Company*, the Sage Creek Ranch still ran about 6,000 sheep in 1968.

Lincoln hired on with Koch as bookkeeper in 1968 and toured all the company's holdings to familiarize himself with ranch operations.

He offers the following description of the Sage Creek country: "The source of the stream called Sage Creek is about twenty miles north of the Sage Creek Camp (ranch headquarters) in the foothills of Ben Holt Mesa. Ben Holt is a high, bald mountain plateau about 8,000 feet in elevation, or perhaps a little higher....I have been there in July and had to wear a jacket in the middle of a sunny day. Ben Holt is one of those places where the magnificence of Nature flows into a person's soul.

"...Sage Creek runs through a series of sub-irrigated meadows past the Sage Creek Camp into Red Rock River and then into Clarke Canyon Reservoir. Sub-irrigated means that the groundwater level is so near the surface that plant roots dip into constantly saturated soil. It takes a special type of plant to grow in this marshy situation. Water would be only two or three feet below ground level and in some places even standing on the ground. In these conditions grass produces a lot of forage and many animals can be concentrated here. These sub-irrigated meadows are known as the McKnight Meadows, probably named for some homesteader who lived here. His log cabin still stands, although it is in poor condition. I can remember helping Marion Cross (former foreman at Sage Creek) drive a small group of sheep into it so we could catch them and load them into a trailer."

CRACKED LEATHER AND GHOST COWBOYS

During the heyday of the Cooke Sheep Company, the stage road ran right by the headquarters' front steps. The ranch sustained residency as an independent community, with its own commissary, saddle shop and livery stable. The Sage Creek Ranch now provides a home to foreman Gary Mills, his wife Beckie, their two children and a few cowboys.

Gary and Becky Mills, Sage Creek Ranch.

Beckie, Gary and the kids live in the old headquarters, a two-story, wood-frame house. The cowboys reside next door in the former company store.

North of the headquarters is the saddle shop and harness room. Old slick-fork, high-back saddles still line the walls and work benches. It was Constructed as a garage shop where buggies and wagons could be driven in and fixed, and most saddle repairs took place upstairs. Walking into the shop, seeing and touching all the old saddles and smelling dried, cracked leather, gives one a sense of living history.

If the visitor stands long enough in the dimly-lit shop, he or she can almost hear an old ghost cowboy telling the saddle maker just how he wants that seat built up or how that stirrup got busted when a colt broke through a fence. Across the old stage road, the cavernous 100-year-old livery stable and barn still stand. Gary and the hands saddle up in the 50-horse barn. The old tie stalls still serve cowboys on roundups, when Gary puts on lots of extra help.

Forty-two-year-old Gary has worked on more than 22 ranches. He says he should have known better than to hire on with an outfit that has electric lights in the barn.

"Lots of cowboys won't work at a ranch that has a barn with lights. They say the boss works you twice as long and you never get a chance to sleep."

Winter mornings, cold-backed horses and freezing saddles are nothing new to Gary. Born in Colorado, he grew up in Wyoming, where during high school, he cowboyed at the Antlers Ranch near Meeteetse. Gary and Beckie, both adopted children, in a twist of fate that seems foreordained, both bore the Mills name, though their families were unrelated. The couple married right out of high school. After twenty years they have a 19-year-old son and an 8-year-old adopted son. Since our visit Gary has been promoted to cowboss and he and Becky have moved to the Beaverhead ranch near Dillon (see page 73).

BIKERS AND BLACK HATS

Gary and Beckie's story typifies young cowboying couples. While he worked on ranches, she often cooked. "I started cooking for haying and shipping crews," Beckie says. "I graduated to relief cook and started cooking odd-hour meals. On one ranch the regular cook prepared meals at 6 a.m., noon and 6 p.m. Cowboys don't necessarily keep such fixed schedules, so I started filling in on those days when they worked early or late. I've cooked breakfast at 3 o'clock in the morning and dinner at 10 p.m."

On most ranches with small crews, such as Sage Creek, the boss hires extra help for special occasions such as brandings and gatherings, which makes life on the range and in the kitchen pretty hectic.

On one ranch, Gary recalls, he mined coal to make ends meet. He worked the graveyard shift and still worked days on the ranch. During branding, he came home one morning and found the yard full of bikers that the boss had hired.

"None of that `motorsickle' gang had ever done a lick of ranch work before and the calves pretty much got the best of them," Gary says. "Even the big, burly, mean-looking guys got flattened a time or two. They might have created havoc on the highways, but they didn't know a thing about wrestling calves."

Big ranches hire large farm labor crews in addition to the regular cowboys. The two work groups banter amongst themselves. Cowboys don't like to dirty their hands working on machinery, and farmers think that a cowboy is useless because he just rides all day while the horse does all the work.

On some ranches, cowboys won't eat with farm hands and farm hands won't sleep in the same building with cowboys. On the Desert Land and Livestock Ranch where Beckie and Gary worked near Woodruff, Utah, this cowboy controversy came to a head. Beckie still smiles every time she tells the story.

"One summer five young teen-age hands hired on the farm crew. They all wore cowboy garb and tried to act tough, like they were real, honest-to-God cowboys. They all had big, black, western-style hats and the cowboys called 'em `The Black Hats.'

"The Black Hats kept talking about how easy cowboying was, so Ed, the cowboss, talked to the farm foreman and borrowed those boys to help move some cattle.

"The farm boss knew what was up and gave his okay. At 4 o'clock the next morning, they saddled up and came in for breakfast. I packed their lunches and off they went. They had to move 800 head of cows and calves from one pasture to another during a 25-mile drive that ended up being more like 60."

"The calves tired and started hanging back, and the cows got mad and started running back to the ranch. The whole bunch just proved to be really tough to move."

By nature, calves stay near their birthplace. If left alone, they rarely venture more than a few hundred yards from this safe spot. If driven, they instinctively return to this area. A cowboy has to understand cattle to move cows with young calves. The cowboy must be well-mounted and able to ride with great control to move the bunch slowly as one unit. "By 10 a.m.," Beckie continues, "the Black Hats were not only tired of chasing cows, but they were saddle sore and sick of eating dust. Two of the boys fell off their horses and threw up their breakfast. They were a sick, sore and sorry outfit.

"But there was no turning back. The pickups and horse trailers were still ten miles away and the boss wanted those cows moved—today!

"Gary retrieved a coat and two catch ropes that The Black Hats lost along the way. At 6 p.m. they reached their lakeside destination. Nobody had eaten or drunk since breakfast. Gary rode back for the pickup that still had their lunches. The Black Hats were so hot and thirsty that they plunged off their horses and wallowed in the water with the cows.

"After the calves were mothered up, the rest of the cowboy crew rode down the hill to the trucks at a full gallop, just a whooping and hollering. They wanted to show the Black Hats that cowboys do this kind of stuff on a daily basis. They all got home about 10 p.m. and I had a big dinner waiting. Even though I had cooked T-bones and 'taters, only two Black Hats showed up to eat. That was the last we heard from the Black Hats about cowboying being so easy."

BAKED TURKEYS AND BREAD AS HARD AS HOCKEY PUCKS

When Gary and Beckie first married, she says she couldn't boil water without burning it, and her bread turned out hard as a hockey puck. "Now, homemade bread is what I do best," she says. "Gary told me he loved me because of my bread. I appreciate that compliment, but I hope that's not the only reason."

Beckie's baking skills have proven useful in other ways. She once baked 25 live turkeys.

The Millses worked on a horse ranch where Gary raised some turkeys. One day it poured rain. Turkey chicks drown in just a little water, and they lost nine birds before Gary could herd them into the house.

"We wanted to save them all," Beckie says. "They're good at killing rattlesnakes. We couldn't figure out how to dry a drenched turkey, so we decided to put 'em in the oven. We set it at 150 degrees and left the door open. They dried and survived. That was the only time I ever baked turkey and never got to eat any."

'Motorsickle' gangs, Black Hat Boys, bread as hard as hockey pucks and turkey tales—Gary and Beckie insist they live a routine life. They believe in old-time values, like offering a helping hand to anyone in need, although their favors sometimes backfire. Beckie laughs when she tells about one favor that boomeranged.

Gary once worked at a Colorado feedlot where they castrated young bulls and threw away the testicles. Gary kept a bunch, brought them home and Beckie fried up a batch of Rocky Mountain oysters.

The next day Gary took some to work for his lunch. His fellow workers gobbled them up, because they tasted so good. Never again did the feedlot hands allow those bull testicles to be thrown away. "We never got any more for ourselves," says Beckie.

Beckie throws away or wastes little at Sage Creek. The Millses must drive 60 miles to the nearest shopping center in Dillon. Beckie has learned to plan ahead and make do with what's on hand. Her small, comfortable kitchen adjoins a dining room where she, Gary, the kids and their crew take their meals.

On the back porch, hands shed overboots, hats and coats, or get dressed out of the weather once they finish their meal. Every full-course meal, served and enjoyed in a family atmosphere with the Millses, is just like Sunday on the farm. Beckie and Gary say grace before eating and table talk revolves around cattle, horses, weather and grass.

Beckie never turns away a visitor and always seems to have just enough food for everyone to have an extra helping. She learned long ago to prepare plenty, but never throw anything out. Beckie and Gary have learned to conserve by going through hard times.

During the winter of 1979-80, Beckie recalls, they were snowbound during a 128-inch blizzard. They made little money for groceries, although Beckie fed Gary, their oldest son, and a hired man.

"This old cowboy had been at the ranch for over fifteen years," Beckie says. "He kept eggs frozen for times like this. I'd borrow eggs from him and we'd separate the yolk from the white to make the eggs last longer."

Beckie's Baked Slug

There's probably a pretty good story behind Beckie's "Baked Slug." Although we don't know what that story is, we guarantee it tastes better than it sounds.

1 pound hamburger meat
½ cup finely-chopped onion
¼ cup catsup
¼ tablespoon ground black pepper
1 10½-ounce can cream of mushroom soup
2 cups flour
¾ cup yellow cornmeal
2 tablespoons baking powder
½ tablespoon salt
1 tablespoon curry powder
⅓ cup shortening
¾ cup milk

Brown the beef and onion. Drain off the grease. Add the catsup, pepper, and soup.

In a separate bowl, mix the flour, cornmeal, baking powder, salt and curry powder. Add the shortening, and cut in until the mixture is crumbly. Add the milk (use more, if desired).

Turn onto a floured board and knead 10-12 times. Roll out into a 12" square. Spread with meat mixture. Roll in a jelly-roll fashion. Cut into slices and place on a greased pan.

Bake at 400 degrees F. for 20-30 minutes.

Serve with brown gravy.

Serves: 4

OHRMANN RANCH
FLINT CREEK VALLEY, MONTANA

FORTY YEARS OF COWS AND CALVES
Phyllis Ohrmann, Creative Cook

In the north section of Flint Creek Valley along Highway 10 near Hall in western Montana, a sign informs the traveler he or she is approaching the Ohrmann Ranch. Complete with a metal cutout of an Angus bull and an artist's palette, this notification perfectly describes cowboy artist and rancher Bill Ohrmann and his wife Phyllis.

For more than 40 years the Ohrmanns have run their registered Black Angus cow/calf operation on 1,000 acres of irrigated land. Cow/calf and breeding operations typify many western ranches these days, producing more than just beef on the hoof.

A rancher has to be mighty savvy in order to introduce his bulls to his cows at exactly the right time. At the end of their nine-month gestation period, the mother cows must drop their calves during the time of year most advantageous to ranch operations and to the herd's survival and health.

The Ohrmanns have about 65 cows. Each year they sell their bull calves and bred heifers. Calving begins around the end of January and lasts four or five weeks. In April, branding occurs, and each fall, sometimes as late as November, the Ohrmanns hold a production sale for other ranchers to come and purchase prime Ohrmann stock to improve their own herds.

BILL'S ALLEGORICAL ANIMALS

As the ranch sign indicates, not only are the Ohrmanns dedicated cattle ranchers, but Bill Ohrmann fulfills another side of his personality through his art. Until the early 1970s sculpting had been merely a hobby Bill pursued for relaxation.

Now he's gained a national reputation as an artist. Bill's work has been accepted several times for exhibition during the renowned Charles M. Russell Show, held in the famous artist's Great Falls hometown each March. He has also shown at Spokane's prestigious Museum of Native American Cultures (MONAC) during the annual western and wildlife exhibit, and he's won a number of Best-of-Show awards at various art exhibitions.

Many of his bronze and polyform sculptures express his fascination with wildlife, and some of his work details his preoccupation with the cowboy life.

"He's a close observer of animals and their habits," Phyllis says of her cowboy/artist husband. "He knows how to capture them; his accuracy makes his work especially good."

Bill also sculpts 2'- to 3'-high wooden pieces picturing strange animals that play a part in his own personal mythology.

"Not everyone appreciates these allegorical works, because I don't think they really understand them," Phyllis says. A quiet man, Bill doesn't talk about his work much or the meaning of these animals that inhabit his own personal landscape.

Bill continues to develop long-term relationships with his art clients. He met a collector one year when the fellow came to hunt in the Flint Creek Valley, and they've continued their business relationship since. In addition, Bill is in demand as a teacher and art demonstrator. He gives classes, and exhibits at galleries and shows throughout the state.

Bill's not the only creative type in the Ohrmann household. Phyllis devises her own recipes from scratch, and enjoys her cooking experiments.

NOT MUCH OF A BOX COOK

"I'm not much of a box cook," she says. While Bill was born about a wagon ride from their current ranch, Phyllis was brought up on a 300-acre farm near Wadena, Minnesota where her folks raised corn, small grain, milk cows, pigs and chickens. Phyllis says Minnesota winters helped prepare her for weather in the Flint Creek Valley. With the help and encouragement of her mom, a 4-H leader, Phyllis participated in many of the organization's kitchen projects. Early in her life she gained baking experience from cakes to breads.

That early kitchen experience has stood Phyllis in good stead since the days when she met Bill. His sister introduced her to her future husband during a Western summer vacation from her Minnesota teaching position.

"When I first met Bill, I probably didn't appreciate art as much as I do now," Phyllis says. She's learned a lot since then about sculpture, and she's also gained much valuable kitchen experience.

For over 40 years since they were married, Phyllis has prepared meals for Bill and their three children who are grown now, but who still live in the area. Their son still lives at home and works on the ranch, freeing Bill to pursue his art.

Her wild rice casserole has become an Ohrmann family favorite. Once, only the Chippewa Indians harvested the tall aquatic plants from Minnesota lakes. Savory and dusky, wild rice has become somewhat more available in recent years. The search to acquire wild rice for this dish will be well worth the trouble.

Ohrmann's Wild Rice Delight Casserole

1 cup wild rice

1½ to 2 pounds hamburger meat

2 onions, chopped

1 cup chopped celery

1 can mushrooms, drained

1 can water chestnuts, drained, chopped

2 10½-ounce cans mushroom soup

Rinse the rice. Cover with 3 cups water and cook 45-55 minutes or until tender. Brown beef and drain off the grease. Saute the chopped onions and celery in with the beef. Mix the rice, onions and celery. Add the drained mushrooms, chestnuts and soup.

Bake at 350 degrees F. for 30 to 45 minutes.

Serves: 2-4 people.

FLYING D RANCH
GALLATIN GATEWAY, MONTANA

WHERE TIME HAS ALMOST PASSED BY
Vera Spring, Reluctant Ranch Cook

Sitting with Sam and Vera Spring in their comfortable living room listening to them talk about the old days, even the most casual visitor can tell they've played a part in a unique chapter of the Western experience—ranch life around World War II emphasized the cowboy's role. Machinery occupied much less of a position in ranch work than it does today, and many cowboys stayed with their outfits until they retired.

In Sam's case, his old ranch has even furnished him a house in the little town of Gallatin Gateway (population, about 500), one of those places that time has almost passed by.

Fifteen miles from Bozeman, but a million miles from modern-day life, Gallatin Gateway has its classic Main Street with general store, cafe, bar, local garage, hardware store and assorted shops. Conspicuous for their absence, national chain stores have not yet discovered Main Street.

People hereabouts dress in working cowboy gear, and ranch life is still the norm. In fact, Gallatin Gateway has maintained its cowboy lifestyle to such a degree that movies such as *Montana* with Richard Crenna and Gena Rowlands, have been filmed here.

About a block from Main Street, Vera and Sam sit in their living room discussing how

Sam Spring (second from right) with the Flying D cowboys in the 1960s.

cowboy life has changed. While Sam has retired from the Flying D Ranch where he's worked since the late 1940s, he still cowboys for nearly eight months a year, including a stint from July to October, when he runs a cow camp in Gallatin Canyon for the Sappington Ranch.

NOTHING BUT A SHEEPHERDER WITH HIS BRAINS KNOCKED OUT

"A cowboy's nothing but a sheepherder with his brains knocked out," Sam laughs. But he laments the disappearance of an old work ethic alive when cowboys showed loyalty to their ranch and rode for the brand. Sam's pride in being a cowpuncher is very apparent when he talks about how times have changed.

"Sam can't walk a lick," Vera says of her husband. "But he'll walk two miles to catch a horse just to ride one mile." That's the ultimate compliment to give to a cowboy.

As fourth-generation Montana cowboy and author Spike Van Cleve said, "If God had wanted a man to walk, he would have given him four legs."

Today, ranching, like many other modern concerns, has become just a business, offering temporary employment for transients who drift from job to job with no pride in their work, Sam says. Vera, however, thinks maybe the old days were not so great in some ways.

Of French Canadian descent, she grew up in the remote and ruggedly scenic section of Montana near Polebridge, on the western boundary of Glacier National Park—a country filled with towering peaks and U-shaped glacial valleys, refuge for nearly every large North American mammal, including the grizzly bear and timber wolf. There, sage-covered prairies surround dense western red cedar and ponderosa stands.

Vera's folks homesteaded in the Polebridge area. She learned to ride horses, trap, and work cattle when she was a girl. Her mother tried to teach her how to cook, but gave up.

"I did everything I could to stay out of the kitchen," Vera says. She liked being out-of-doors, doing activities that were not considered ladylike, but were part of everyday survival. In fact, Vera wanted to be a cowhand and not a ranch cook. But folks in those days considered her ambitions no life for a lady.

"When I grew up, women were never allowed around the barn or the bunkhouse where the men were," Vera says. Rigid role divisions between the sexes and a society that emphasized social control kept women from being cowgirls. But Vera believes many women make just as good hands as the men.

Today, many more cowgirls than in the past now work on the range, side by side with their male counterparts. All-gal crews travel from ranch to ranch and hire on for short periods to do seasonal chores. These cowgirls have gained acceptance, not because they're women, but because they do their jobs well.

Such acceptance certainly was not the case back in 1946 when Vera met Sam. They both worked on the Nine Quarter Circle Ranch just north of Yellowstone Park, owned by pioneer dude ranch operator Howard Kelsey.

Vera had answered an ad to cook for dudes who came from all over the country, and Sam had just returned from Burma, where for five years during World War II he broke pack horses for the Chinese artillery. Sam hired on as ranch handyman and wrangler, and it was there that he began to date Vera.

She says Sam's light feet when he danced the cowboy two-step and the waltz attracted her. After a short courtship they married on April 5, 1947.

Sam still claims Vera chased him, though he didn't so much mind being caught.

The next fall they moved to the Flying D, where Sam had worked sporadically since he was a 10-year-old school kid. Sam's grandfather had even homesteaded part of the Flying D, and his father and uncles had cowboyed there.

Every youngster who has grown up on a ranch has to make a decision when he or she comes of age; either a young man or woman rejects the cowboy way of life and decides to leave for good, or he or she chooses to continue the traditions practiced by thousands of ranch families who for generations have cowboyed throughout the West.

Cowboying was in Sam's blood and he decided to follow in his family's bootsteps. For

Vera, her childhood in the saddle hardly prepared her for her career.

She cooked at the Flying D from 1968 until Sam retired in 1982. When asked to take this position, she turned the job down flat. No way would this hardy gal from Polebridge, Montana be trapped behind a stove. After the ranch manager and several hands begged and pleaded with her, Vera agreed to cook for two weeks at the Flying D.

As often happens with reluctant ranch cooks, those two short weeks turned into 15 years.

"I hate to cook...I really hate to cook," Vera says. But recalling her life on the Flying D where her cooking won her great popularity and respect from the hands, she says even all that cooking was not so bad. "Besides," she says, "I

Sam Spring, retired cowboss of the Flying D during branding in the late 1970s.

had a saddle and a horse. I rode whenever I wanted."

Vera's written a poem about the Flying D crew and her years seeing all the hands and their various food preferences. Today she most certainly would hire on as a cowgirl, and a damn fine one, too.

Vera Spring's Chicken Supreme

One 3-pound chicken fryer, cut up
½ onion, minced
½ cup finely chopped celery
½ cup minced parsley
½ tablespoon ground sage
½ tablespoon ground savory
1 tablespoon salt
Dash of ground black pepper
2 cups fine bread crumbs
½ cup melted margarine
¾ cup flour
4 cups broth
6 eggs, beaten

Cover the chicken with water, and cook until tender. Cool, remove meat from bones and reserve the broth.

Sauté the onion in a little margarine. Add the celery, parsley, sage, savory, salt, pepper and 1⅓ cups bread crumbs. Place the mixture in a greased baking pan and place the chicken on top.

Blend the ½ cup margarine and flour. Slowly add the broth, stirring constantly. Cook for 5-10 minutes, cool, add the eggs, and pour over the chicken. Sprinkle with remaining bread crumbs. Bake at 350 degrees F. for an hour, or until thoroughly heated.

Serves: 4

Vera Spring with one of her favorite horses.

THE COWBOYS FROM THE FLYING D
by Vera Spring

The year just passed has been a blast
I'm sure we'll all agree,
And here are a few of the things we do
That other people see.
Sausage brown will rate a frown
Watermelon he won't touch.
Mark eats beans and most things green
But he won't eat very much.
In early spring strawberries and cream
Is something Bob likes best.
If he has biscuits and gravy, then just maybe
He will forget the rest.
"I want to eat. Where is the meat?"
Says Roland, loud and clear.
"I won't eat sprouts, so throw them out.
Pass the 'taters here."
And then there's Jack, and it's a fact
He will eat most any fare
Except one thing and that's ice cream,
For this he does not care.
There are very few that won't eat stew
Nor eat an apple pie.
But for our Chuck, they are bunk
And he'd rather pass them by.
"I won't eat rice at any price.
Make that coffee strong!"
If it's not stout, Sam will throw it out
Then beller loud and long.
"There's just one thing, I don't like cream,"
Says Stewart with a frown.
"If it won't whip, I think I'll skip
Dessert this time around."
George likes steaks and sourdough pancakes.
Bread pudding is a must.
He likes country fries, sweet cherry pies.
He will even eat the crust!
Beans and ham, dinner rolls and jam,
He always eats French toast.
He likes maple bars, but girls with cars
Is what Monty likes the most.
Larry packed his gear and left last year
He told us all, "Goodbye."
We heard him say as he rode away,
"I'll be back for chocolate pie."

BUGLI RANCH
STEVENSVILLE, MONTANA

A TASTE OF ITALY IN MONTANA
Shirley Bugli

The Bitterroot Valley of western Montana is often described as one of the most beautiful places in the entire state. And in Montana, that is really saying something. This is an area of contrasts, with rolling sub-alpine woodlands of ponderosa pine, Douglas fir, larch and aspen, and the magnificent bitterroot, the flower for which the valley and the mountains have been named. The plant was the food staple for the Lewis and Clark expedition in 1805 and 1806 when they traveled through the valley. The two explorers had learned the value of the plant from the Salish Indians who lived in the valley at that time. The Salish, as did many other Plateau tribes, valued the bitterroot on a par with the camas, an edible plant with a large root also found in the area.

The Indians moved each May to the mountains to gather a supply that would last for the year. There are stories that a bag of dried bitterroot was worth as much as a horse. The plant has 12 to 18 white or pink petals, and grows on the rocky slopes of a bare mountainside.

As with so many other things that have changed, there are people who have lived all their lives in the Bitterroot Valley and have never seen the flower, now the state flower. Civilization has squeezed the habitat for the flower so that each year it gets increasingly more difficult to find.

But the jagged glacial peaks are still there, and the Bitterroot National Forest, extending into Idaho, covers 1,577,883 acres and is headquartered in Hamilton, Montana, just down the road from Stevensville. With the towering peaks of the Bitterroot Range to the west, and the Sapphire Mountains to the east, this is the valley used by Chief Joseph as part of the escape route for the Nez Perce Indians in 1877 as they fled the U.S. Army on their failed attempt to reach Canada.

Nestled in the northern part of the valley is Stevensville, the first white settlement in the state, sometimes referred to as the Plymouth Rock of Montana. The community dates back to 1841, when Father Pierre Jean DeSmet came to set up missions among the Salish Indians who were living on the valley floor along the Bitterroot River. The original mission is now the oldest in the Pacific Northwest, and is open to the public.

Today, throughout the Stevensville area and the rest of the valley, there are small farms and ranches, lots of cattle and horses, and Shirley Bugli's fine Italian cooking.

One of the best family outfits is the Bugli Ranch on the Sunset Bench south and east of town, where they raise cattle, good quarter horses and Christmas trees. Shirley and Zack Bugli are both natives of the area, and both have roots firmly planted in the land. Shirley's love for the country has always been strong. She remembers her reaction when, as a young girl, she moved with her family to Hamilton, the county seat.

"I couldn't stand city life. I didn't even like to go to the movies. I wanted to get on my horse and go for a ride," she says. The love of the outdoors and animals is a theme that is probably a part of every real Westerner's makeup. Everyone wants to surround themselves with horses, dogs, and other assorted animals rather than the trappings of city life. They make life on a ranch, which can be far from other people, easy to abide.

Although Hamilton was not exactly a big town—by the 1990 census, it still only had a population of 2,700 people—to Shirley, that was the big city.

"I grew up riding, being around animals, spending time outside, and loving every minute of it." The natural beauty and serenity of the area where Shirley grew up is overwhelming. As we sit in her kitchen and look across the valley to the towering peaks of the Bitterroots and the open farm and meadowland on the Sunset Bench, you can easily understand why Shirley and Zack have stayed at the ranch since the 1950s. It would be hard to find better land with a better view. And the country must be good for one's health, because today Shirley is a grandmother, active horsewoman, and still never misses a branding or roundup.

The Buglis met in high school and married in 1949 shortly after graduation. By 1953 they had decided that they loved the ranch life, and it was time to get their own place and begin to raise a family.

They've been at the ranch at the Sunset Bench, located below the Sapphire Mountains, on Bugli Lane ever since, enduring hard times and enjoying the good times. And they've watched the area grow. The population of Ravalli County seems to double each decade as farms and ranches are cut up into small acreage for retirees and "hobby" ranches.

This growth, which the developers call progress, but others call an intrusion into a lifestyle, has taken away some of the friendliness and informality of the valley. Now neighbors are not quite so neighborly, and the strain caused by demands on county services is almost reaching to the breaking point. The agrarian base is suffering from erosion, a trend that is gaining in many of the more scenic valleys' of the West.

SIMPLER DAYS FROM THE PAST

Shirley thinks that the rural life was simpler and more personal when she and Zack first settled at the ranch. She remembers the times when a local kid would be baking a cake, and if Mom wasn't home, a call would be made to the local telephone operator to ask her to call back in 30 minutes so the youngster wouldn't forget to take the cake out of the oven. And the operator in those days would gladly do it for the young baker— whom she probably knew. Often that operator was Shirley herself!

There are three Bugli children—two girls and a boy—who all worked on the ranch, and rodeoed in high school and college. Today, grown and married with children of their own, they are still involved, raising and training horses, cattle ranching, farming, and maintaining the family's ties to the land.

The oldest daughter, Lynette, with her husband Tony and daughter Elaine, ranch just down the road from Shirley and Zack. They raise cattle and show-quality paint horses and pony jumpers. Their daughter Elaine, a teenager, is already a champion show rider. Shirley, daughter Lynette, and granddaughter Elaine did some team penning, a relatively new sport that requires a team of three riders to pen three marked cattle in under two minutes. The three Bugli gals managed to take first place. Second-oldest daughter Vonnie, who lives with her three teenage daughters, just across the road from Lynette and Tony, is a noted horse trainer and gives clinics throughout Montana. Jay, the youngest Bugli, is a helicopter mechanic, but lives very close by with his wife and two young children, so he is always available to help at brandings, roundups, and other stress times that happen at a ranch.

Shirley has to cook for many people at the ranch—her husband, the kids, their many friends and all of the people who love to come to the ranch and help at brandings and roundup. But she never complains. In fact, she says she really enjoys cooking. Back when Lynette and Vonnie were on the rodeo team at the University of Montana, the Bugli Ranch was a gathering spot for team members, and Shirley often treated the young cowboys and cowgirls to a great meal. She has learned lots of recipes over the years, but is quick to add, "When you marry an Italian, you have to turn Italian." That means cooking Italian dishes.

UNDERCOVER COOKING

Shirley learned to cook Zack's favorite Italian meals by "spying" on his mother, who was French, but who had learned Italian cooking from Zack's dad. Italian cooking has become a favorite with the three Bugli children. The girls recall having to "scrub to the elbows" before they could even help out with the pasta in the kitchen, one of the central gathering spots at the Bugli Ranch, where on a cold winter day it is warm and friendly around a wood-burning stove.

When she's not cooking pasta, Shirley likes to cook beef dishes. She is a very, very active member of the local chapter of W.I.F.E., Women Involved In Farm Economics, a national women's organization devoted to promoting the use of beef and preserving the cattle industry and ranching. She is also a serious political activist, often appearing at hearings and writing letters, all on behalf of protecting the water and land rights of ranchers and others involved in agriculture from the encroachment of developers, recreational users, government organizations, and any others who might threaten the livelihood and way of life that is so precious to her family and friends. As she so often says, "You always have to keep alert, because you never know what these people are going to try next."

Gnocchi

3 eggs
½ cup water
1 teaspoon salt
1 tablespoon grated Parmesan cheese
3 cups flour
1 cup mashed potatoes
butter

Beat the eggs with the water. Add the salt and grated Parmesan cheese. Mix this in with the flour and mashed potatoes. If the dough is too soft, add more flour. If it is too stiff to work with your hands or is crumbly, add more water.

Roll with your hand to a roll about 2 inches in circumference. You will have a long roll. Cut with a knife into ½-inch pieces and then roll each of these pieces in your hand until each is about the size of your finger. Press your thumb in the center to make sure you have a consistency for cooking.

Boil in a large kettle in salted water, the same as any other pasta. Cook until tender. Drain. Put in a large bowl and add generous amounts of butter and sprinkle with Parmesan cheese. Pour over it a generous amount of your favorite meat or spaghetti sauce.

SHELTON RANCHES
GALLATIN GATEWAY, MONTANA

TED TURNER TAKES OVER
Mary Noyes, Cook With a View

North of Yellowstone National Park and west of the college town of Bozeman, Montana, the Shelton Ranches have been home to purebred Santa Gertrudis and Salier cattle, crossbred range cattle, and one of the best stories of cowboy romance and cowboy cooking you'll ever come across.

The Shelton Ranches used to have their main headquarters in Kerrville, Texas. Shelton had bought the old Spanish Creek Ranch in Montana, once owned by the world-famous King Ranch, also headquartered in Texas. It has been apretty common practice for large ranch corporations to have holdings in a variety of states, mostly for tax purposes, to save on shipping costs and to breed cattle to adapt to various climates.

The King Ranch used the Montana location to breed their northern herd of Santa Gertrudis cattle, a breed developed on their ranch in Texas by crossing Brahman cattle with shorthorns to produce a big, strong red critter that was officially recognized by the United States Department of Agriculture as a breed in 1940. The Montana herd was bred to handle the colder weather of the northern states. Bobby Shelton added the historic Flying D to form his Montana ranch operation, one of the largest in the south-central part of the state.

Recently, Ted Turner, the TV mogul, bought the ranches from Bobby Shelton and has taken all of the cattle off of the range and replaced them with buffalo. This has taken some time, as it will have to be determined what the carrying capacity of the range is for buffalo while developing a herd. It has created an unsettling situation for many of the cowboys, who now don't know what their futures hold. Most don't have the slightest idea of how to work buffalo.

Out by Cherry Creek, a long way from town, the Noyes family lives a typical ranch life at the former headquarters of the Flying D.

COWBOY ROMANCE AND COWBOY COOKING

Dan is a top-notch cowboy, and Mary is the camp cook. But they didn't start out as cowboy and cook. Not by a long shot. When Dan was still a teenager, he went to visit Mary's dad to borrow an old roping horse. After using the horse, he returned to borrow a horse trailer. And because he took such good care of the equipment, and because they were both left-handed ropers, Dan and Mary's dad seemed to develop a special bond. For those of you who don't rope, it might be of interest to know that ropes are coiled for either a left hander or a right-hander, and most good cow ponies are trained for roping off one side or the other.

Mary thought this young cowboy was "kind of cute," and eventually Mary and Dan started to date. Mary laughs very affectionately when she says, "First the horse, then the trailer, then the daughter." It seems that cowboys sure do have their priorities in order.

When Dan was just 19, he got a cowboy job at the Shelton Ranch. As Mary describes it, "Dan got the job in October, and we either got married in December, or we didn't get married at all 'cause of calving, branding and gathering. I didn't want to wait a year, so we gave everyone about three weeks' notice we were goin' to have a wedding." And Dan and Mary got married!

Now in their mid-30's, they came to the Shelton Ranch in 1976. They've seen lots of cowboys come and go in that time. Mary says they get applications from all kinds of guys from all over the country, and some are even from foreign countries. She adds that many of the applicants are so well-educated that they almost qualify as veterinarians, and then there are those "that have been sitting at a desk and don't even know which end of a horse is which...a little experience goes a long way in getting a job here."

Some of these dudes looking for a job sound a lot like the fellows in the movie *City Slickers*, just wanting to get away from their urban environment but with no real idea of what they are getting into or any sense of making a commitment to the life. Mary also thinks that too many of the guys who apply for cowboy jobs are really playing at being cowboys, and don't take the work seriously.

Not too long ago the real cowboys came and stayed for years. Now they usually stay for a year or so and then move on. Some of this can be attributed to the fact that large corporate ranches have become fairly impersonal—places where there is very little real concern for the individual cowboy.

And some of the lack of stability is due to low pay and very unsteady work, except for the best cowboys. In addition, some of the constant moving around is just the natural attrition of guys who never really wanted to be cowboys, but just went West to "find themselves" or have another of life's experiences.

There are still some men and women who romanticize the cowboy life and believe, as Anthony Trollope, the English novelist, wrote in 1862 about the West, that there is "...a certain manliness about its men, which gives them a dignity of their own...It seems to me that no race of men requires less outward assistance than these pioneers of civilization."

Maybe once, but not so anymore. Most ranches, particularly those in the north, have little all-year work. With calving and branding in the spring, and sorting and shipping in the fall, winter is mostly a time for making sure that the water tanks aren't frozen solid and that the hay is fed out to the cattle and horses each day. This is very demanding and far from romantic work.

In winter the work gets done day in and day out, even when the temperatures reach 35 degrees below zero, and the wind chill factor gets down to 80 below. The cows are pregnant, the bulls have been separated from the herd and are off by themselves, and the few hands are kept busy by simple chores, certainly not enough to keep a full crew in the bunkhouse.

The work gets to be tedious and a real burden. Heck, in Montana the ground is frozen so deep you can't even drive in a new fence post.

When Dan and Mary first moved to the ranch, Mary worked in town while Dan earned his paycheck as a cowboy. Several years ago, after living in three different dwellings on the ranch, a really nice house at Cherry Creek Camp became available. The one drawback to this house for Mary was that part of the house also served as the cookhouse for that section of the ranch. The manager offered Dan and Mary the house, but only if Mary could be talked into being the camp cook. She remembers, "I didn't care about cooking."

The location of the Cherry Creek Camp wasn't too bad, either. Almost surrounded by the Gallatin and Beaverhead National Forests, the mountains are some of the most rugged in Montana, a state noted for its mountain scenery. There are the Madison and Gallatin ranges, the Absaroka and Beartooth, and to the north, the Bridgers. The area is also a haven for trout fishermen, hunters, hikers and skiers. And just for size, the Gallatin National Forest contains 1,735,239 acres; the Beaverhead is even bigger, with 2,147,500 acres.

Cooking three meals a day starting at 6 a.m. is a big job at Cherry Creek. During the spring branding, the calves are given their shots, the bull calves are castrated to make them steers, and all of the herd is given the ranch brand. Mary has to cook for about 17 hungry and tired cowboys—punchers who work from sunup to sundown until the work is finished. As she says, cooking for a crew like this is "just short of an assembly line. We keep 'em moving, almost like a buffet." During the winter months, when the big crews are laid off, Mary cooks for about eight men.

This all seems to suggest that Mary Noyes learned to cook as a young girl, and developed her recipes and techniques over a long period of time. But that is just not the case. In fact, she never did learn to cook at home, and had to learn to cook as sort of on-the-job training. The things some people will do to keep a nice house in a beautiful location!

Coffee Cake

This cake is best if made the night before and baked in the morning.

18 to 20 frozen rolls (Rhodes preferred)
ground cinnamon
1 3-ounce package Jell-O vanilla pudding,
(the kind you cook)
½ cup margarine
½ cup light brown sugar

Arrange the rolls in a bundt or 10-inch tube pan that has been sprayed with Pam or oiled. Sprinkle with cinnamon and pour the dry pudding mix over the top.

Melt the margarine and stir in the brown sugar. Cook until blended. Pour over the rolls and let sit overnight at room temperature.

Bake for 25 to 30 minutes at 350 degrees F.

Yield: 18-20

BEAVERHEAD RANCH
DILLON, MONTANA

MATADORS OF THE RANGE
Jackie Cross, Backup Cook

Folks around Dillon, Montana call the large ranch south of town up Blacktail Deer Creek the Matador, and all the cowboys there are known as Matadors. They wear that name with pride. The ranch is owned by the Matador Cattle Company, which also owns the Matador Ranch in Texas and at one time owned the Roberts Ranch in Wyoming, the Jack Young Ranch in South Dakota, the Garvey Ranch in Nevada, the Clabber Hill Ranch in New Mexico, and the Webster Ranch and White Ranch in Texas.

The Matador Cattle Company was put together by Fred Koch, an M.I.T.-educated Texas ranch-raised engineer who invented the oil distillation process that came to be known as the Winkler-Koch Cracking Process. The units were sold around the world and Koch became a very wealthy man. In about 1940 he began buying ranches to diversify his holdings, and purchased the Beaverhead Ranch in Montana in 1951.

The ranch was started by a couple of Scottish immigrants, Phil Poindexter and William C. Orr Sr., and was originally known as the P & O. The two men were partners in the cattle business in Siskiyou County, California. In 1865, during the height of the

Beaverhead ranch cowboys flank a calf as Sue Marxer brings the hot iron.

73

Montana gold rush, Bill Orr trailed 400 head of steers up to southwestern Montana and delivered them to Conrad Kohrs in Deer Lodge Valley.

Conrad Kohrs, one of the founders of the cattle industry in Montana territory, got his start by buying trail cattle, fattening them up and selling them to the miners in the nearby boom towns. Kohrs built one of the largest ranches in the Big Sky state, and today the Grant-Kohrs ranch is a national historical site operated as a living museum and run by the National Park Service. It is maintained as close to the original as possible and is open to the public.

After Orr delivered the steers to Kohrs, he stayed around awhile and looked over the good grass country that he saw in Montana. He was so impressed with the productivity of the area, he filed on some land south of present-day Dillon along Blacktail Deer Creek. It is interesting to note that the area, probably because of the severity of the winters, was never permanently occupied by prehistoric people. The Shoshone, Nez Perce and Blackfoot Indians visited here in the summer to hunt, fish and gather berries. The Shoshone named the valley the Beaverhead, after a large rock resembling a beaver's head that sits near the river of the same name.

Sacajawea, the Shoshone Indian guide of the Lewis and Clark expedition, remembered the rock from her childhood and led the explorers into the valley because she wanted to find her people. In 1805, the party spent several days here and hunted and rested before resuming their westward journey.

EARLY STORM AND LOST CATTLE

The story around Dillon goes that when Poindexter and Orr first entered the Beaverhead Valley with their cattle, they were hit by an early fall snowstorm and the herd split up and couldn't be located. The owners returned to California and gave the animals up for dead, but the next spring found the herd along the Blacktail Deer Creek, not only alive and well, but fat and slick. The Scottish cattlemen were convinced that here would be a good place to ranch. For the next two years they trailed cattle up from California, a trip of over 1,500 miles. They built a headquarters for the ranch and registered the first brand in Montana, the square and compass, the insignia of the Scottish Freemasons.

The ranch operated as the P&O for over seventy years and was a forefounder of the cattle business in Beaverhead County. Today, the Beaverhead Ranch still operates under the square and compass logo and turns out some of the best beef in the world. Writing in his book, *Rich Grass And Sweet Water, Ranch Life With The Koch Matador Cattle Company* (Texas A&M University Press, 1989), John Lincoln, who started out as bookkeeper and retired as president of the company, writes: "The Beaverhead Ranch was, of all Fred Koch's ranches, the greatest source of pride to him and it continues to be to his family and many of the Matador employees.

"The 257,000-acre ranch is the largest in Beaverhead County, Montana. When you drive down a road that runs southeast from Dillon, after eight miles the pavement ends and the Beaverhead Ranch begins. Although it is out of sight, Blacktail Deer Creek is only a quarter of a mile away, on the left, flowing toward Dillon and the Beaverhead River.

"Three miles off to the right is a high mountain ridge called the Blacktail Mountains. From these mountains, Sheep Creek flows into Blacktail Deer Creek. The headquarters of the ranch is at the base of the Blacktail Mountains. A graded dirt road proceeds up the valley more or less parallel to Blacktail Deer Creek. On each side of the road large fields of alfalfa and barley are irrigated by these two creeks. Two miles from pavement's end is the ranch headquarters.

The manager of the Beaverhead Ranch is Marion Cross, and he has been with the company since 1959. Marion says that the ranch runs straight Hereford cattle and he likes it that way. "We tried Brangus bulls to cross with our cows," he said, "but it just didn't work out. We find we do better if we stick with good Hereford bulls on our Hereford cows."

Ray Marxer, the cowboss, agrees. "Marion and I look at a lot of bulls each year. We drive a lot of miles and we cull a lot of critters. We're real particular about the kind of steer we want to turn out for the market. We're real interested in something that will sell and something the housewife will buy."

Ray knows cowboys and horses as well as he knows cattle, and has been with the ranch since 1974. He, like Marion, was foreman at the company's Sage Creek Ranch when he was twenty-one years old. "It was a struggle," he said. "I made a lot of mistakes but the company kept faith in me and kept me on. I'll always be grateful for that."

Ray and his wife Sue have three children and are very happy with life on the Beaverhead. Ray loves to ride, is an excellent roper and gets maximum production out of his cowboys. He says he has the best job in the world and sometimes feels guilty for taking money for doing something he loves so much. Sue rides with Ray when she can and is an accomplished amateur photographer. Her photo of Ray dragging a calf to a branding fire graces the cover of Lincoln's book, and she frequently sells photographs to *Western Horseman Magazine* for their annual calendar. She helps out with the doctoring during branding and fills in as cook once in a while.

MORE HUNGRY MEN THAN SHE COULD COUNT

Jackie Cross, Marion's wife, is also a back-up cook, but has not always enjoyed that luxury. She started cooking for crews when she first married Marion and they were living at Sage Creek, then a sheep operation. "I had only cooked a little as a very young girl," she says, "so I really didn't consider myself a cook when Marion and I were married."

At Sage Creek, Jackie, who hails from Arkansas, where they do things a little slower, learned to cook in a hurry when Marion started bringing in the hired help to dinner. "The first week I was there they threw five men at me to feed," Jackie says. "The next week it was ten, and after that I lost count as I was too busy to keep track."

"I was the only cook there," she continues, "and the only woman within miles. When we started lambing I was cooking six meals a day, seven days a week. Sometimes I would prepare over a hundred sandwiches to send out to the shearing crews. I was barely twenty years old and I told 'em, 'here I am working like a fool and I can't even vote yet.'"

Jackie's nearest neighbor was Ella Tallent, and she gave the young bride some sage advice that helped the novice cook at Sage Creek. "Ella told me that if the men left one bowl empty from the food I served, that was fine; but if they emptied two bowls, I wasn't fixing enough. I remembered that. I also stuck to the basics of meat, potatoes, a vegetable and a dessert. Somehow we all lived through it because I don't recall anyone dying from my cooking."

However, Jackie does remember another helping hand that she got during those first few months at Sage Creek. "A radio station in Idaho Falls, I don't know which one, had a program where they gave out recipes. I heard about it and started getting some good recipes, and my cooking improved considerably."

When we contacted Jackie about interviewing the cook that was employed at the Jake

Camp, she almost came unglued. "Oh no. You don't want to interview that guy. He ain't no real cook. He just calls himself a cook. If you want to interview a real cook, you're welcome to come on over and I'll talk to you, but please stay away from old Dew (the cook at the Jake), he'll just mess up your mind."

We did make the drive to the Jake during spring branding, and Jackie met us there and filled us up with Rocky Mountain oysters, a delicacy for which she is locally famous and which is normally available at branding time. She leaves no doubt that she is a real cook.

She says that once she got the basics of cooking down, she really started liking it. "I like to make bread. Once I started making sourdough, I'd keep two batches going all the time. You've got to keep sourdough fresh. It's taken a lot of time, but I feel real good about my cooking."

Of course, Jackie hasn't always felt good about her cooking, and said that the first time she tried to make bread it came out poorly. How poor was it? "The dog took one whiff of it and walked away. I must have used too much flour or something. Anyhow, it was bad, real bad. I finally figured out how to make bread and now I make lots of it and have fun doing it."

Having fun, it seems, is something Jackie likes to do while cooking. Once she got her kitchen legs under her, she started being more relaxed and productive. But then the equipment didn't always cooperate. "We had an old electric stove that was about worn out, and one day it caught fire. I sent the kids down in the basement to cut off the breaker, but the stove kept smoking and sizzling, and I was afraid it was going to burn the house down. So I grabbed it and heaved it outside."

Not too long after the stove incident, Jackie forgot to set out the meat for a meal. The

Jackie Cross serves up Rocky Mountain Oysters, Beaverhead ranch.

76

crew came in and ate and left and never mentioned the missing dish. "I reckon they'd heard about me moving that stove," she says. Apparently the men didn't want to Cross Mrs. Cross.

Later, on April Fools' day, Jackie decided she'd check the men's memory with a little trick. She didn't put anything on the table at mealtime except crackers and coffee. As expected, the crew came in and sat down and never said a word. Perhaps it was because Marion had a sign up that read "Do your visiting in the bunkhouse." Ranch hands know better than to test the cook. "They never said a word," Jackie says. "They just sat there and stirred their coffee and waited. I've never heard so much coffee stirring in all my life." Marion had to go in and get Jackie over the giggles before she came out with the food.

Running a ranch the size of the Beaverhead is serious business, and Marion does not tolerate much foolishness. Lincoln gives a graphic description of dining at headquarters. "...No one enters the dining room until the cook rings the dinner bell; early arrivals wait on the enclosed front porch. Before ringing the bell, the cook sets the food on tables that are fifteen feet long. If needed, four of these tables are available. Long wooden benches provide seating. After finishing the meal, diners carry their own eating equipment to the kitchen, scrape their plates into a garbage can and stack everything for the cook's convenience. Everyone leaves the table upon finishing the meal, and there is not much lounging over coffee and cigarettes. When the last diner leaves, the kitchen is closed until the next meal...The cook is a privileged person on the ranch and receives a lot of respect and consideration."

While Jackie may play a trick on the hands now and then, she is very serious in her praise of them. "These guys are great to cook for. They'll eat about anything you set before them." Well, almost anything.

"I have to look out for them, though. Some of them don't have very good teeth and some don't have any teeth. I asked one of the men once, 'where are your teeth?' 'Gracie's got 'em,' he said. He had hocked his false teeth."

Jackie sends a couple of recipes that you sure can sink your teeth into, providing you've got any. Besides being a sourdough expert, she is famous for her Rocky Mountain oysters and puts on a big feed of them during the ranch's annual Christmas party. If you haven't tried this old ranch recipe, do so the first chance you get. The way Jackie fixes 'em, they melt in your mouth and you won't even need teeth.

Rocky Mountain Oysters

1 dozen calf testicles

2 eggs

½ can evaporated milk (undiluted)

2 cups flour

2 tablespoons salt

½ tablespoon pepper

1 cup vegetable oil

When testicles are removed, drop them in a bucket with clean, cold water.

Clean off outside skin, wash and freeze. When ready to prepare, partially thaw, skin and remove the "oyster." In one bowl, beat the eggs and add milk. In another bowl mix flour, salt and pepper. Dip the "oysters" in egg mix, then in flour mix and drop into hot (350 degrees) vegetable oil. Fry "oysters" until they turn golden brown; remove, cool and serve.

LYON'S RANCH
DRUMMOND, MONTANA

HOME OF THE BULLSHIPPERS
Jim Snead, Rancher, Cook and Doctor of Horse Psychology

About fifty miles east of Missoula along I-90 up the Clark Fork River, highway travelers top out on a hill, remnants of an extinct volcano, where a billboard reads, "Welcome To Drummond, Montana, Home Of World Famous Bullshippers."

The sign sets a tone for Drummond, population 200—time and the Interstate have bypassed the little town. Ranching and logging still provide the primary income for area residents.

Folks thought building the Interstate highway would kill Drummond. Then most of the railroad crews pulled out, and people said that Drummond was dead for sure.

Like the hardy ranchers, cowboys, loggers and miners that live around there, somehow Drummond has survived, although they've gone from five to three restaurants.

Drummond's a two-bar town. Swede's Place serves as unofficial town hall, where local types gather to exchange news and gossip, and the Canyon Bar provides an unofficial employment office for the community. Drummond is a working person's town.

A mile west of town, by the highway, Jim and Katherine Snead's 5,000-acre Lyon's Ranch runs mixed-breed commercial cattle and registered American quarter horses.

Katherine's father managed the ranch for over forty years as a dairy operation. Mr. Lyon took great pleasure and pride in his huge two-story white barn, his sparkling-clean milking shed and his acres of lodgepole corrals and pens.

CARS WERE SLOW AND
AIRPLANES FEW AND FAR BETWEEN

But Mr. Lyon's greatest pride came from his pampered Morgan horses. He let his mares and colts run free on the open ridges behind his house, and he loved showing his Morgans. People around Drummond say they never had seen anyone so crazy about horses as old man Lyon, that is, until Jim Snead showed up in town.

Born in Alamo, New Mexico in 1920, Jim says, "Cars were slow and airplanes few and far between." As far back as he can remember Jim's been a working man. He's been around livestock his whole life, but he has a special way with horses. Jim Snead is a horseman's horseman. He's learned about life from his horses and his work, not from formal schooling.

In his youth, his folks, like parents of most rural families he knew, struggled to eke out an existence in the desolate high plains of eastern New Mexico. To help feed his family, Jim began, as a boy of eight, breaking horses at $4.00 a head.

"A lot of money in them times," he says. "Levis were $2.00 a pair and boots were plumb out of sight."

In those days, bronc busters "cowboyed them horses down," as Jim says. As a boy, Snead hadn't the brute strength needed to overpower, subdue and break a horse.

He believes a horse responds to positive training, rather than fear of human domination.

Jim Snead tried a new method that he calls "gentling them easy-like."

Snead ran an unbroken horse into a round corral, roped him, and gradually managed to close-tie the animal to a snubbing post in the center of the corral, where he stroked and rubbed the wary "bronc" over its entire body, until the horse learned that man meant him no harm.

At that time of bronc busters and horse breakers, Snead pioneered a whole new way of training horses. He also improved Old West training methods. Even today many horse trainers still feel that in the training process, a young horse must be subdued, broken and conquered. Many cowboys still bust horses in the New West.

But in Jim Snead's nearly three-quarters of a century as a horse trainer, he has found that trying to conquer a horse leads to abuse, and the animal develops bad habits from his negative association with man.

"Don't pick a fight with them colts. Love them, and make them think you're their daddy," that's Jim's credo.

Developed in New Mexico, Snead's horse training methods proved popular, and by the time he was 14, Jim had so many horses to train that he dropped out of school. The school superintendent called Jim into his office to explain to this young cowboy that without an education, he would never amount to much.

"I listened to him a while," Snead recalls. "Then I asked him how much money he made." When the superintendent told him the amount, Snead replied, "Well, Sir, I make more money than that right now a-breaking horses."

A DOCTOR OF HORSE PSYCHOLOGY

Jim left school without further discussion, and ended his formal education, but that moment also marked the beginning of his doctorate in horse psychology. Jim left home and went about 30 miles to the Waggoner Brothers' Ranch at Santa Rosa, one of the largest cattle outfits in the country, with both Texas and New Mexico holdings that turned out some of the finest horses in the world.

Jim helped out on a road-building crew for his first ranch job, operating a horse-drawn front-end loader called a fresno.

"I was too small for that job," he said. "Every time the bucket hit a rock or bump, the handles lifted me right off the ground. But I stuck with it until they made me quit."

This boy from Alamo impressed Waggoner Ranch manager Coleman Morehouse with his tenacity.

"He just kind of adopted me," Snead says of Morehouse.

Jim worked for Morehouse off and on for more than 20 years. Snead coached Morehouse's daughter in cow cutting until she took a state championship. Jim produced some million-dollar horses.

Later, Jim got his own ranch and trained horses for actress Greer Garson, who owned a nearby New Mexico ranch.

In the mid '60s, a lawyer friend moved to Hamilton, Montana and wrote to his old roping buddy about how green the grass was in Big Sky country. This enticement got to be more than Snead could stand.

On the New Mexico plains, Snead says, a cow had to graze at 10 miles per hour to get a belly full of grass. And, as in Texas, horses didn't get much bigger than sheep, because of the hot sun and the sparse grass. Jim Snead moved north.

He first settled in western Montana's Bitterroot Valley, north of Hamilton. He built up a little horse ranch, but the locals didn't seem to have much horse sense, according to Snead.

"There's mostly forty-cow farmers over there," he says with thinly-veiled contempt. "They don't know what the hell a good horse is for. I've seen 'em time and again chase cattle into a pen, then tie their horses to the fence and work cattle afoot. They're heavy-handed mechanics in the Bitterroot. All they know is jerk and spur training and they wouldn't last five minutes on a good horse ranch."

So Snead started wandering, and his marriage began to disintegrate. His travels took him to Drummond and to the Lyon's Ranch. Here he found a home. Mr. Lyon was in failing health, and Jim Snead began to care for the old man who shared his love of horses. People in Drummond say Jim Snead packed Mr. Lyon around everywhere he went—to the grocery store, horse shows and sales, until the old man's final days. His doctors amputated Lyon's legs, but even that couldn't keep him from his beloved Morgans.

After Mr. Lyon's death, Katherine and Jim married, and Jim managed the ranch. The old cowboy had no interest in dairy farming, and because he loved quarter horses, he sold the Morgans. The entire direction of the Lyon's Ranch changed under Jim's management.

EVER THE OLD COWBOY

Snead, ever the old cowboy, spends most of his waking hours around the hundred-year-old two-story frame ranch house, once a showplace, which has now been converted into a bunkhouse. Jim has built a sleek, modern brick ranch house for Katherine that occupies a position below the bunkhouse on a hillside overlooking the highway and the Clark Fork Valley.

To approach the bunkhouse, a visitor must exit I-90, go under the underpass and drive back west along the highway. A washed-out gravel driveway takes the visitor up a slight hill past chicken pens and horse corrals into a barnyard encapsulated by buildings, much like an old European courtyard.

A new arrival, when exiting his vehicle, must exercise caution. A passel of growling dogs of every shape and variety usually greets the interloper, although these canines never carry out their vicious threats. As far as we know, Jim owned only one dog that bit. He kept that cur chained to an elm tree and built a dog house of hay bales, where he banished the unruly critter.

From the courtyard, a guest enters the bunkhouse through a small back porch where Jim stores firewood and dog food. Inside, ten-foot ceilings and sixty-year-old wiring, plumbing and heating await the guest's inspection. Most activity centers on the 30-by-15-foot kitchen-dining room, furnished with throw-away furniture and army surplus eating utensils.

Cowboys and ranch hands sleep both downstairs and upstairs in any of six bedrooms. There's no heat upstairs and some of the mattresses haven't been aired out since gas was 10 cents a gallon.

We remember one hand who even slept in a barn stall with a litter of pups. He went by the name Slim. When Snead let him go, Slim later returned to sleep in the barn and almost burned it down.

Jim Snead has a kind heart, and habitually picks up transients who work on the ranch for awhile in return for room and board. Some are pretty fair workers, down and out on their luck; but others, if they lived in town, would be known as bums, and yet others are downright dangerous.

One winter we hired on with Snead to break some colts and hung around 'til spring branding. Our little adventure resembled Keystone Cops Branding Calves. The motley crew varied from some excellent cowboys to some real know-nothing roustabouts.

That hodgepodge group let cows jump in the river, and dragged calves through creeks, branding the cattle upside down and backwards. The Lyon's corral was a real zoo. Old man Lyon surely spun in his grave.

But looking back, our crew proved great fun. Snead took us all to Swede's for chicken dinner and we had a great laugh. Jim just loves people too much to hold a grudge for any length of time. He's had his share of trouble, though. A few years ago a ranch logging accident killed his youngest son, Sam, the pride of his life. Snead never recovered from this blow. The ranch has never been the same.

A BUCKING SON OF A GUN

Jim always runs his mares in the same country where Lyon ran his Morgans. The hills take off right behind the corrals. A stout walker can climb for hours before reaching the top, where private property joins Forest Service lease land. Cattle and horses do well up here, especially horses. Snead leaves them there all winter and they learn to shift for themselves.

The colts learn to watch their footing and they develop large lungs and strong legs from running free. The young horses learn to watch cows and not to fear every rustle in the woods.

Jim Snead learned to cook in a roundabout way. Before his first cowboying job with Morehouse, Snead hired on at the Vivian Ranch, which is about halfway between Roswell and Fort Sumner.

He started out as a bronc buster. One day he was riding a "pretty spooky colt." The boss pulled into the yard with a wagon and a team of mules. The rattling wagon scared the colt.

"That little son of a gun commenced bucking and jumped right into that team of mules," Jim says. "My knee hit the end of the wagon tongue and I felt something give. I knew I was hurt, but I didn't know how bad."

A crippled cowboy ain't much good around a ranch, but ranchers know that riders get hurt and they always take care of their own. As soon as young Jim could hobble around, he became the cook's helper.

"That cook was an old Mexican," Jim says. "And he liked to have worked me to death. I've never had to work so hard in all my life. There was always something needing to be done. I cut wood. I hauled wood. I built fires. I cooked stews and I washed pots and pans—all on one good leg."

The lessons learned from that Mexican cook have stayed with Jim all his remaining years. In spite of the hard work he put in at that outdoor kitchen, Jim still loves to cook. As a ranch owner/operator now, Jim doesn't have to cook, but his reward comes from doing a great job. In the old ranch house, Jim cooks on a rare half wood-burning, half gas-fired Magic Chef.

"This old stove reminds me of me," Jim says. "It's old and tough and has some character." Snead coaxes wonderful results out of his old stove. "I don't know how old she is," he says as he wipes a fleck of soot off the white enamel surface, "but I gave $300 for that stove 15 years ago and only the good Lord knows how many years it had been used before that." Snead has mastered his old Magic Chef the way he learned to master colts long ago in New Mexico.

He said he learned from watching old Mexican hands whose secrets were passed down by the Spanish. In his youth he also read horse training books by Professor Jesse Berry, and he says, "I don't want to brag on myself, and I don't want to make anybody mad at me, but I don't think there's anyone in the world who understands horses better than I do. I talk their language! They understand me! I psychology them horses and they do just about anything I want."

Jim Snead's the kind of man who makes the West western. He's tough on the outside but he believes in people. He's learned a lot about life, this doctor of horse psychology—Snead's knowledge didn't come from schooling or books, but from experience, as tough as the desert winds or the hard Montana winters. If you think you can out-psychology Jim Snead, think again. He's got more layers to him than an onion; Jim Snead's an enigma, just like the Western weather, a rare breed of man who is fast fading from the scene. His kind will be sorely missed.

Jim Snead's Beef and Veggie Breakfast

4 medium potatoes, peeled, sliced and cooked.
2 tablespoons vegetable oil
1 pound hamburger meat
1 16-ounce can whole kernel corn
1 cup diced green peppers
1 cup diced onions
1 16-ounce can stewed tomatoes
6 large eggs

Fry the potatoes in the oil. Cover the pan and add 1 tablespoon water occasionally to keep the spuds moist so they steam and don't burn. Stir frequently.

In another pan, crumble the burger into small pieces and cook until done, add to the potatoes. When the potatoes and burger are done to taste, add the corn, peppers, onion and tomatoes. Simmer for 10 minutes. Stir in the eggs and scramble all the ingredients.

Serves: 6.

Jim Snead riding "Setting Up D," checking cows on his ranch.

82

Big Hole Grazing Association
Wisdom, Montana

Going Back to Basics
Pete Schroeder, Cowboy, Cook

Throughout the West, many grazing associations formed over a hundred years ago, when small ranchers joined their cattle in common herds and turned them onto government lands to graze pastures normally only available to large, corporate outfits. Associations then hired a cowboy or two, depending on the number of cattle they ran, to ride herd on their livestock during grazing season.

Herding cattle differs from driving them. When cowboys herd livestock, they simply stay with them day and night, moving them slowly from pasture to pasture.

Herding cattle is the quintessential cowboy's job, requiring living with the cattle every single day and looking after their welfare. Herding is a lonesome job that means long hours in the saddle and a lot of dedication. But the work has its rewards.

Big Hole Grazing Association cowboy Pete Schroeder says he looks forward each year to being alone with the cattle, his horses, mules and dogs.

Raised in Boise, Idaho, Pete never even saw a cow until he was about 10 years old. His dad got him a job on a ranch, so that the city boy would have something to do during the summer and perhaps learn about hard work.

Young Pete took to ranch life like deer to an alfalfa field. "I loved it," he said. "The ranch was near wilderness and had lots of animals, and I really liked that."

However, the ranch also had lots of rattlesnakes and Pete wasn't too crazy about snakes. On one occasion, they killed 17 rattlers in a quarter-mile of trail. Pete says he was glad he was on horseback.

Pete joined the Marines at 17 and served as an infantryman in Vietnam and as embassy guard in Saudi Arabia and Beirut, Lebanon. Wounded twice in Vietnam, he received two Purple Hearts and was recommended for the Silver Star for bravery.

"That was quite a deal," he says of his combat experiences. "I was just a kid, but you grow up in a hurry in a war."

Pete liked the Marines and stayed for eight years. He would have remained for 30 but couldn't advance in the infantry. "I was a grunt," he said. "And once you're a grunt, you're always a grunt. I just got tired of it, so I got out. To hell with it. I figured I'd try something new."

He returned to Boise and worked for Air Idaho, a local airline that failed. He then worked for another company that also went under. Finally he went to Boise State University for a couple of years.

"I was a typical restless kid," he said. "I was trying to find myself."

In bumming around, Pete met an old-time cowman, Roy Rouark, who owned a ranch near Boise.

"I got to helping old Roy," Pete says. "We'd fix fences and do some riding and work cattle. I found that being back around animals was very peaceful for me. After 'Nam I'd get tensed up pretty easy and I was just happier around livestock."

Pete picked up a couple of horses and started day work for nearby ranches. Then he got a full-time riding job with the Bennett Brothers Cattle Company.

"I quit when they asked me to put up hay," Pete says. "I ain't got nothing against haying. I just don't like crawling under machinery and getting all greasy and dirty."

Pete learned the do's and don'ts of the trade pretty quickly. He left Bennett's and rode with the Gold Fork Grazing Association near the ski resort town of McCall, in Sun Valley, Idaho. But ever the restless cowboy, Pete decided to move on.

"I was married at the time," he says, "and it wasn't working out so good. I was a full-grown man but still pretty young in the mind." Pete split with his wife and left Sun Valley, but he didn't give up cowboying and he didn't give up on marriage.

"A man ain't meant to be alone," he says. "Even a cowboy needs someone to love."

Pete took a job caretaking at a ranch where he trained horses in summer and gave skiing lessons during the winter. "I finally felt that my life was starting to come together again," Pete says. In Challis, Idaho, Pete met and married a pretty young schoolteacher. This marriage is one of the happiest events of his life.

"We got married on the Fourth of July and didn't even have a place to live." Pete found a ranch job on Fourth of July Creek. His life stabilized and he began to relax. "Dee's real good to me," he says. "She understands me and we get along real well together."

On Fourth of July Creek Pete trained and collected horses and a few mules. He also taught skiing at Lost Trail Ski Area on the Continental Divide near the Montana-Idaho

Pete Schroeder and his mules; Big Hole Grazing Association.

84

border. Here he met skier-cowboy Dennis Smith, Big Hole Grazing Association foreman. Dennis lives on the headquarters ranch east of Wisdom. Dennis and Pete discovered they had a lot in common, and Dennis had an opening for a rider. So the next spring, Pete and Dee moved to the grazing association's ranch on the marshy, grassy plains of the Big Hole Valley.

"I really like the Big Hole," Pete says. "Dennis left me alone with my stock, and I could do my work and nobody bothered me. It's a slow pace over there. I really like that."

Several Beaverhead County ranchers belong to the Big Hole Grazing Association that owns the headquarters ranch, and leases other land to run cattle in summer and fall.

One lease pasture stretches from McVey Creek, north of Wisdom, east to the Pioneer Mountains. Another pasture runs east of the Big Hole Battlefield ten miles south of Wisdom. The association ships cattle by truck to the McVey Creek pasture in early May. They move their cows over Highway 43 through Wisdom to the south pasture in June and push up-road to forested pastures in July.

McVey pasture typifies western rangeland, with rolling hills covered by sagebrush and bunch grass. The pasture slopes up toward the east into ponderosa-covered ridges with good native grass growing in shaded meadows. The high and dry, sage-shrouded south pasture lies opposite a wide, boggy swamp that feeds Ruby Creek. Native grass grows tall in sub-irrigated meadows, and the mosquitoes grow big as bumblebees in the ranch's wide, flat pastures along Lake Creek.

One old-time hand said that Big Hole mosquitoes can bite through a bale of hay. But the grass is excellent and the cattle grow fat before being moved to the high country.

The association's mountain pastures run for about 12 miles along each side of 43, from just south of the Battlefield to the Continental Divide. The 7,000-foot-plus Bitterroot Mountains trap snowfall in winter and spring, releasing water in summer, nourishing the sweet, native grass that grows tall and strong. The cattle gather in groups of 200-300 cows, calves and herd bulls. Each rancher keeps separate herds until all the cows breed. Then, as the weather gets hot and the grass shortens in the lower pastures, the cattle bunch for the mountain drive.

They trail past the Big Hole Battlefield, where in August 1877, Nez Perce warriors defeated Col. John Gibbon's soldiers and held them under fire, while Chief Joseph escaped with the surviving women, children and horses. Now, under supervision of the National Park Service, the Big Hole Battlefield is a national monument, a peaceful place where elk, deer, moose and bear wander through trees that once hid frightened soldiers from Indians incensed by the murder of their women and children while they slept.

After the cattle settle on their summer range along Chief Joseph Creek, Pete and Dee put up a canvas tent, complete with folding cots and wood-burning stove, prepared to spend the summer following the herd. Little by little, cows, calves and bulls roam in small bunches and find their own special meadows where they browse, sleep and fight flies.

A COWBOY'S DREAM COME TRUE

"Riding for the Big Hole Grazing Association is a cowboy's dream come true," Pete says. "In the mornings it's crisp and cold, and I get up before daylight and do my riding and checking before it gets hot. Around lunchtime I take a nap. Afternoons I can go fishing. In the cool of the evening I ride once more and see that the cattle are safe and secure before I turn in for the night. There's always work to be done, but there's no big hurry about it." Dennis stays at headquarters and takes care of any cattle and horses there, checking up on Pete and Dee weekly when he brings mail, groceries and other supplies. As they push the cattle higher into new pastures, the riders have to pack in salt. Slowly the herd moves from one section to another, until it tops the Divide around October. Then snow begins to fall, and the cowboy must ride the ridges and coulees, rounding up and pushing the strays back to the valley floor for the trip home.

In late summer, Dee returns to her teaching job in Florence. Poor old Pete has to tough it out alone in the Big Hole.

Dutch Oven Secrets of a Cowboy Cook

"I usually don't eat breakfast," Pete says. "I grab a cup of coffee while I'm dressing, then I saddle a horse and I'm gone. Later I'll start a stew or roast in a Dutch oven. I really like to play around with my Dutch ovens. I've got five in different sizes and I want to get a whole set. I'm kind of a cast iron nut. You can't beat 'em for cooking."

As a small boy, Pete started helping his mother in the kitchen. She let him bake cookies and bread and made sure that he didn't ruin the kitchen or kill off the family with his recipes.

His parents both worked full-time, so Pete began cooking evening meals.

"By the time I was twelve, I could prepare whole meals," he says. "I'd come home from school and cook dinner. When the folks got home from work, everything would be ready to eat."

Pete further honed his cooking skills after he got out of the Marines. He was chef at the Boise Holiday Inn for a while and also cooked in a couple of large restaurants while going to college. "I can make quiche and all that fancy stuff, but I don't really fix that out here (on the range). I need real food, and I don't like to eat out of a can, so I do a lot of real cooking." Pete calls steak and potatoes, roast, fish, chicken and wild game real food. In season, he likes to roast grouse with carrots and celery in his Dutch oven. "One big meal like that will hold me all day," he said. "It ain't no trouble to eat good. People just make a big project out of it. They're afraid of making mistakes, so they settle for a bunch of junk."

Pete says that people don't use Dutch ovens because they're afraid of them. He says that the iron pots are just like a casserole dish, and a cook uses similar methods when cooking with them.

"Dutch ovens are so versatile," says Pete. "You can cook with them on top of the stove, in the oven, on an open fire and under the flames. I know of no other utensil you can do that with. I cook stews, steaks, roasts and even popcorn."

According to Pete, the secret of Dutch oven cooking rests in caring for the utensil. "Be gentle with her," Pete says. "Wash her with mild detergent and don't scrub. Wipe her clean and never soak her in dishwater." Made of porous metal, Dutch ovens absorb materials quickly, he cautions.

"Don't use salty oils; they'll ruin your oven. Mostly taking care of a Dutch oven relies on common sense," he said. "I don't mind taking care of my Dutch ovens because they turn out such fine food. I like to eat good food. I don't care for junk."

Most old cowboy cooks swear by sourdough as a cooking standard. Not Pete, though. He says cowboy bread's too much trouble. "You have to keep sourdough at a certain temperature or it won't work. Down here in the Big Hole, even in the summer, it gets down below freezing at night. Sourdough has to be kept warm to keep working."

Old-time wagon cooks kept sourdough starter in their bedrolls to keep the yeast active. They went to a lot of extra effort keeping bread starter alive, because without starter they had no bread. Today's ranch cooks have prepared dough.

The greatest invention in the world, according to Pete, is Bisquick, which tastes great and makes beautiful biscuits.

"There ain't a thing wrong with it," Pete says. "I use it all the time."

Pete says the old preference for sourdough among cowboy cooks reminds him of the argument amongst cowboys about their horses. "Some guys won't ride a mare. But I've got one that is the best horse in the world. She'll just work her heart out for you. I wouldn't trade her for anything." While many cowboys keep riding their geldings and preferring their sourdough, Pete sticks by his mare and swears by his Bisquick.

"Dee wants me to go back to school and get a degree, and I reckon I should," he said. "But right now I'll stick with cowboying. I love the freedom. I love animals. I love cooking and I love riding. I've got the best of two worlds and I think I'll enjoy it while I can."

Pete's Dutch Oven Casserole

2 pounds round steak
⅓ cup flour
2 tablespoons vegetable oil
1 1-pound can small whole onions,
drain and save water
1 10½-ounce can cream of mushroom soup
1 10½-ounce can water
½ teaspoon salt
⅛ teaspoon ground black pepper
1 teaspoon seasoning salt or paprika

Roll the steak in the flour and pound until the flour coats both sides well. Cut meat into small pieces and brown in the oil in a Dutch oven. Remove the meat and keep warm; add the onions, cream of mushroom soup, 1 can of water, salt, pepper and seasoning salt to the meat.

Make a gravy from the meat drippings and water from the onions. Add the meat and onions back into the Dutch oven and bake at 350 degrees F. until meat is tender, about one hour. Sprinkle with seasoning salt or paprika before serving.

Serves 4 to 6

Dumplings For Pete's Dutch Oven Casserole

1 cup bread crumbs
¼ cup melted butter
2 cups sifted enriched flour
4 teaspoons baking powder
1 teaspoon poultry seasoning
1 teaspoon celery seeds
1 teaspoon poppy seeds
1 teaspoon dry onion flakes
1 cup milk
¼ cup vegetable oil

Mix the bread crumbs and butter together and set aside. Sift the flour, baking powder, and poultry seasoning. Stir in the celery seeds, poppy seeds, and onion flakes.

Combine the milk and oil. Make a well in the flour mixture and pour in the milk mixture.

Pete Schroeder's Cowboy Potatoes

1 pound sausage or hamburger meat

2 cubes beef bouillon (to be used in the hamburger)

4 or 5 medium potatoes, sliced

1 large onion, sliced

1 cup water

1 10½-ounce can cream of mushroom soup

1 clove garlic, minced

paprika, salt and pepper

Brown the meat with the bouillon in Dutch oven or casserole pan. Add the potatoes and onion to the meat. Add the water, soup, and spices, and bring to a boil. Turn down heat and simmer until the 'taters are soft.

If you're feeling brave or hungry, you can add sour cream, cheddar cheese, dried hot peppers and peas. Makes a meal that'll last you all day.

Serves 3-5 people

In parts of Montana, the old ways are proudly preserved.

Section III:
The Great American
Southwest Desert

Money, or lack of it, was the least of the cowboy's worries; independence and the dignity of his vocations was all. He was a horseman, which gave him pride...His string of saddle horses was his utmost concern—for without a good mount, a good cowboy is no cowboy at all. If he could find a paying job, what the hell! And if he couldn't, what the hell!

John L. Sinclair,
Cowboy Riding Country,
University of New Mexico Press, 1982.

New Mexico and Arizona have probably done more to help us visualize and identify with the American cowboy and his world than any of the other western states. Maybe because so many television series, feature films and commercials have been shot in the Southwest, particularly around Old Tucson and Santa Fe, the land seems mythically bound with the Old West as portrayed by Hollywood.

In truth, much cowboy lore developed in these deserts and mountains first explored by the Spanish in the 1530s. This, of course, is the land of Billy the Kid, the OK Corral, all the great Apache warriors, the Buffalo soldiers, the Navajo and their majestic country, Elfego Baca, the Lost Dutchman Mine and many more places, people and events that have blended Western myth and reality.

When each of us saw the Southwest separately for the first time many years ago, this landscape looked very familiar. Ever since Old Tucson was created in 1939 as a set for the motion picture *Arizona* starring Jean Arthur and William Holden, well over 100 films have been shot there. These pictures were the films we grew up watching on Saturdays at the neighborhood movie house.

And, if you are like we are, you've rented them from your local video store. Great movies such as John Wayne's classics, *Rio Lobo, Rio Bravo,* and *McClintock,* Clint Eastwood's *Joe Kidd* and *The Outlaw Josie Wales,* Kirk Douglas' *Posse* and *Shootout at the OK Corral,* and television series, including *Little House on the Prairie* and *High Chaparral—* all were filmed in Old Tucson, just twelve miles west of present-day downtown Tucson. And near Santa Fe, scores of films, like *Silverado, The Young Riders,* and *City Slickers,* and even the Montana scenes in the epic western *Lonesome Dove,* were all shot in New Mexico.

To identify all the commercials made in these two states would be as daunting a chore as listing most of the major corporations and products in America and across the globe. Film crews seem always to be crawling over the New Mexico and Arizona deserts and mountains. But cowboy traditions are more than mere celluloid fictions, existing way before there even was a Hollywood or television. Ranking fifth and sixth in geographical area, New Mexico and Arizona are still sparsely populated deserts and high alpine forests, with mild winter temperatures in the south, and winter tough enough in the northern parts of the states to make two Montana cowboys feel right at home.

Although late to proclaim statehood (Arizona was separated from New Mexico Territory in 1863 and both territories became states in 1912), their history of both Native Americans and European invaders is about the longest in North America. Some of the first evidence of man on this continent was found in the northeast corner of New Mexico, and the traditions of the Anasazi, Mogollon and Hohokam peoples, the ancestors of many New Mexico and Arizona present-day tribes, go well back over 1,500 years. The European invasion came in the 1530s when the Spanish came up the Rio Grande Valley and established Santa Fe as a provincial capital. Today, the "City Different," as it likes to be called, remains the oldest continuous government seat in the United States. And with that settlement, the Indians, Spanish and later Anglo cultures became forever woven into a cloth that has defined the Southwest in every aspect of life.

Clothing, food, language, architecture, artistic sensibility and many other facets of Southwest lifestyle have been influenced by this intermingling of cultures. The romantic notion of the cowboy isn't always at odds with the cowboy's own romantic idea of his life. And such romance may even be more true today. But the cowboy's adherence to a "Code of the West," his sense of pride in his work and his individualism are all real aspects of cowboy living.

Many young men and women choose the cowboy life today because they want to participate in these romantic traditions that are so hard to find in modern life. The cowboy has a love of language. One of the most popular writers for old-time cowboys was and is Shakespeare—not that cowpokes understood everything the bard said, but cowboys loved the sound of his words, the rich texture and rhythm that is closely associated with the cowboy's own colorful speech and his dedication to theatre. For cowboys, a traveling theatre troupe hitting town was a big event that brought some entertainment to the otherwise routine life on the range.

They rode miles and often days to get to town for a good show. And these actors and actresses never played to more appreciative audiences. Many cowboys had little or no schooling and many could not read, so spoken language became a heightened form of communication, and storytelling of any kind became a high art.

The colorful language of the West combined this great mixture of cultures and traditions that existed on the range after the Civil War, where free Negroes, Indians, Spanish and men from many other countries, including those from Europe, cast their fates on the open ranges of the Southwest.

In the vast expanses of the Southwest, where the scenery is overpowering and the brightness of the desert light can dazzle and blind, cowboys wound up slowly but surely developing their own unique ways of getting their work done, something of a combination of Texas cowboy tradition and the rich and ever-present Spanish heritage. The Great Plains, Southern Rockies and Great Basin meet in New Mexico. Elevations range from 2,800 to more than 13,000 feet, encompassing six of the seven life zones, from Lower Sonoran to Arctic-Alpine.

The cowboy had to adapt to these many terrains and climates in order to survive. In Arizona, where elevations range from 100 to 12,670 feet and include spectacular country like the Grand Canyon, Painted Desert, and the Sonoran Desert with its saguaro cactus forests, cowboys had to learn to adjust. Their operating methods, their gear and even their language had to fit these places where they lived, be they Indian, Spanish, Anglo or combinations of all three.

New Mexico and Arizona are still great cowboy states, despite trendy enclaves like Taos and Santa Fe in New Mexico, and Sedona and Scottsdale in Arizona. Even the popular state promotional magazine *Arizona Highways* devotes one issue a year to cowboys and ranching.

Over in New Mexico, around 3,000 member ranches belong to the New Mexico Cattle Growers' Association. And that figure doesn't even include all the sheep and horse ranches or the outfits that don't belong to the state's association.

This land is harsh—or so it seems to the many people who haven't had the opportunity of spending much time in the Southwest. A government surveyor in Arizona reported to Congress in 1858, "The region is altogether valueless. After entering it, there is nothing to do but leave." New Mexico has always been considered the land of "mañana" and "poco tiempo," not closely in tune with the increasingly rapid pace of American industrial life.

Neither state presented much to attract people from the rest of the nation. We mention this singular lack of apparent attraction to emphasize the role the cowboys and ranchers have played in developing this area and the role they still play. Whereas air conditioning made it possible for people to build cities and for retirees to settle here, it was the grit and determination of the cowboys who, as John Guenther wrote, understood a land where "the purple desert flowing endlessly under lonely stars" was, indeed, a treasure.

THE HURT RANCH
HACHITA, NEW MEXICO

SAND, SUN AND JAVELINAS
Minnie Lott, Classic Ranch Cook

The stark, mysterious desert country of southwest New Mexico teems with wildlife, including many a rattler. Even today, parts of this harsh landscape remain unexplored and uninhabited.

The desert is a land of contrasts—from yucca and acacia spread across a great floor, to the rugged, forested peaks of the Pyramid, Hatchet, Little Hatchet and Animas mountains. In a brilliant blue sky the sun radiates through ice-clear air, shining on distant mountains. This is a land of old ranches and proud cowboys.

The Hurt Cattle Company, headquartered in Deming, covers more than 650 sections of deeded and leased land. More than 100 windmills pump water for the thirsty horses and cattle. The current Hurt spread incorporates the old Alamo Hueco Ranch, a 19th-century outfit, and portions of the Diamond A. The ranch extends south to the little town of Antelope Wells and shares a long border with old Mexico.

Day and night, cattle from south of the border cross into the United States at this remote border town where a U.S. 24-hour point of entry has been established to accommodate all the trade. This area once served Apaches led by Cochise and Manga Colorado as a favorite haunt. Today, visitors arrive to hunt the desert wild pig known as the javelina, and other desert game.

Since he was 12, Jim Hurt has been a cowpuncher on this range. With his sons William, Ernie, Lawrence and Avery, Hurt oversees one of the region's largest ranching operations. Jim and his wife Velma live in Deming, New Mexico, where his folks arrived with a wagon and team in 1909 and proceeded to put together a ranching operation. Since those days, the family has ranched, and today, each of his boys lives at one of the various divisions of the ranch.

"My dad's still president of the corporation, and keeps us going," his son William said in an interview with the *New Mexico Stockman Magazine*.

Like other Southwestern ranchers, the Hurts express a deep sense of pride in their contributions that they believe have improved the arid desert land.

"This country would be unusable if the ranchers hadn't come in and improved the land, put in wells, stock tanks, fences, corrals and everything else that makes a ranch operational," Jim Hurt says. "The ranch business in this desert country is real, real difficult. You spend most of your time going into and coming out of droughts."

Jim and his sons know the high desert, and respect this arid and harsh land.

"It's better country than most people realize," one of Jim's boys points out. For those who know this land, the desert can be a productive location for ranching, but these forbidding lands do not relinquish their secrets easily.

The southwestern New Mexico rancher must understand the carrying capacity of his range, and he or she must run cattle bred to withstand the dry, ever-changing desert climate—a climate of extremes. Daytime temperatures may reach the 60's in winter, but drop below freezing minutes after the sun sets. During summer the thermometer may soar above 100 degrees, with heat waves shimmering on the horizon, creating the mirage of a lake in the far distance. Weather moves in with sudden fury that evaporates into blue cloudless skies and brilliant sunlight.

A good rancher runs his stock to avoid stripping away vegetation through overgrazing, which exposes the land to erosion, reduces plant diversification, and promotes the insidious spread of arroyos during flash floods that have carried away much Southwestern topsoil. The desert rancher has to protect water resources, and he must know when to rest areas by rivers and streams where his stock drinks. Jim and his boys do this very well.

The Hurts don't irrigate the land, so they have to depend solely on rain and snowfall to keep the arid grasses productive for their cattle.

Jim prefers Brangus, a Brahman-Angus cross, developed in the 1930s. He bought his first Brangus bull more than 20 years ago, and they've done well because they resist drought more than some breeds, and they move with ease on the big ranges typical of the Southwest. As ranchers often say in praise of the hybrid, Brangus breed at a young age, mother well, and raise stout calves.

The Hurts recently bought breeding stock from the Ladder Ranch near Truth or Consequences to the north and from the Cascabel Cattle Company that has a division by Animas, New Mexico.

Unlike Colorado, Wyoming or Montana, desert ranchers usually don't have to worry about winter blizzards and they don't have to winter feed their cattle. The Hurts leave their bulls out year-round and wean their calves twice a year. Mild winters mean the Hurts have to round up, brand and ship their cattle more frequently than ranches on northern ranges, where calving is scheduled to avoid harsh winter and spring storms.

PART OF A PROUD TRADITION

Minnie Lott cooks for the South Wells division of the Hurt Ranch near Hachita, New Mexico. She partakes of the proud tradition of ranch cooks who are tough minded, yet still care about the cowboys, many of whom are young and far away from home.

She grew up on farms and ranches near Portales, in eastern New Mexico on the Texas border. She started cooking before she began school. At the age of nine, she says, she cooked for 15 hands, and took care of Momma and her new baby at the same time. Minnie still has that same nurturing, watchful attitude toward her ranch crews at the South Wells cookhouse.

Five years ago, when her predecessor started serving red chili and beans three times a day, the desperate management asked Minnie to take the cook's job. Some of the cowboys were picking up and leaving because of the food, which is usually one of the great joys of ranch life. Good food can attract a good crew that wants to stay on, and bad food can drive good hands away. Since wages are low and ranch life is tough, food becomes mighty important.

Meals sure have changed since Minnie Lott took over. If the cowboys fuss about the food, they're finicky eaters, she says, because she offers variety in every meal by serving salads, vegetables, and of course, meat, and she prepares lots of food, so everyone can chow down to his heart's content.

In addition to finicky eaters, Minnie dislikes rattlesnakes in her kitchen. She handles them in her own matter-of-fact style by casually picking up a stick and beating the rattlers to death. She chuckles when she recalls her first snake encounter, when the boys thought she would run off scared and leave them hungry. How little those cowpokes knew Minnie.

"I hate snakes with a passion," she says. "When I see a snake I might freeze and be petrified for a minute, but then I take action. In my kitchen those snakes are on my territory, so they better watch out."

SIMPLE PLEASURES

The ranch cook runs the kitchen to maintain order in what otherwise could be an unruly situation. Making the boys curb their swearing and drinking, and making them mind their manners at meals is not just some prudish imposition on these rough and tough cowboys. Minnie runs a strict kitchen to meet the demands of complex ranch scheduling. Whether it be branding, roundups, shipping or daily work, she must regulate meals to fit into the ranch routine.

Minnie especially enjoys cooking at remote cow camps during roundup season. While in the old days many ranches took out the wagons, today only large outfits with spacious lands still carry on this tradition. Small ranches usually drive herds back to headquarters, where the cattle can be worked in corrals and on branding tables. The large ranches have an advantage in that cowpunchers spend less time traveling back and forth from the home ranch to open range.

At the Hurt Ranch, cowboys have to cover over 650 square miles. Lacking modern conveniences such as electric ranges and refrigerators, modern cow camp cooking evokes the self-sufficiency of bygone days when drovers worked off the back of a horse without the aid of modern machinery, and cowpokes roped and dragged all their calves to a branding fire. For the cowboy purist, camps such as these inspire a sense of wonder and reminiscence for the open range of days past, especially in the hauntingly stark desert of the New Mexico boot heel that has hardly changed since the time of Billy the Kid.

"You get to see country in a way that no tourist ever will," Minnie says.

When a cowboss says, "We'll start at sunup," he means long before first light, and the crew better be stirring to get ready for saddle-up time.

By 4:30 or 5 o'clock in the morning Minnie must have breakfast ready and waiting for the hands. But she never loses her enthusiasm for her work

Minnie Lott in the kitchen at South Wells Ranch of the Hurt Cattle Co. outside Hachita, New Mexico.

and for the life of the open range, even though her tasks seem never-ending; just when one meal ends, preparation for the next begins, while the cook has hardly had time to finish cleanup.

The unrelenting demands of this frantic work schedule never seem to ease up. Order at camp or in the cookhouse mandates a basic rule of law all cowboys must follow, and in return the cook may set out some homemade doughnuts, a pot of fresh coffee or other amenities that make a life of hard outdoor labor seem much more rewarding.

In return for these treats, the crew leaves things as they find them in the cookhouse and refrains from making a mess and creating more work for the cook that will throw her off schedule. The smart cowboy stays clear of incurring a cook's ire through such misdeeds. Some cooks have long memories, and life on the ranch stripped of its few pleasures can be enough to send the hapless cowboy packing down the road.

Out at the ranch, simple pleasures take on a significance that these little comforts don't have for city dwellers. Urbanites take for granted lingering over a hot cup of morning coffee or savoring that last piece of homemade pie after a leisurely dinner. Out on the range, the round of work for hands and cook alike never ends until everyone falls into the sack, bone-weary with exhaustion.

No wonder the boys fight over the last piece of homemade Chess Pie that Minnie baked earlier in the day. Her face flushed with pride from all this attention to her culinary skills, Minnie makes quick work of such arguments by simply claiming the last piece for herself.

Minnie loves to bake so she can evoke the unbridled enthusiasm of the cowboys. She rarely resorts to a cookbook or recipe file. She prepares foods by taste and not by measure, as suits the artist she is. Estimating her Chess Pie recipe Minnie found quite challenging.

Minnie doesn't know where Chess Pie comes from, nor does she know why the dessert bears such a peculiar name. Her interest in the pie lies in more practical realms.

"It's a good pie to take to camp because it sets up real well," Minnie says. She neglects to say Chess Pie is easy to make and great to eat, and is really a pecan pie without the pecans.

Watching a large ranch like the Hurt operation, even a casual observer can see that the ranch cook provides a focus for life out here on the range. Minnie Lott more than measures up as a classic Western ranch cook as she speeds around her kitchen grabbing utensils, pouring, measuring and blending ingredients to her own secret recipes, quick as a bobcat leaping from counter to stove to sink.

Minnie's Chess Pie

1 cup Karo syrup
3 tablespoons margarine
1 cup sugar
3 eggs
2 tablespoons flour
9-inch unbaked pie shell

Beat all the ingredients together and pour into the pie shell. Bake until set, usually 45 to 60 minutes, in a 350-degree oven.
Yield: 1 pie

THE GRAY RANCH
ANIMAS, NEW MEXICO

WESTERN GRASSLANDS
Mary and Danielle Moore, Your Basic Ranch Cooks

Lonnie and Mary Moore both come from old-line New Mexico ranching families. Ranching has been part of their lives since childhood. Lonnie manages the 500-section, 320,000-acre historic Gray Ranch, framed by the Animas Mountains to the east and the Peloncillos to the west, and the Mexican border to the south in New Mexico's rugged, isolated southwest corner. The ranch is south of the village of Animas and was founded in 1843. The traveler must still drive a considerable distance from the northern ranch boundary to the headquarters.

Recently purchased by the Nature Conservancy and then sold to a local group of ranchers, the Gray Ranch is one of the last remaining unadulterated spreads of native Southwest grasslands in the United States. Here, wild animals flourish, and the area remains much as it was in the 18th and 19th centuries: deserted and open range defined by jagged peaks, traversed by few roads.

In 1880 former Texas Ranger Michael Gray gave the ranch his name when, with his two sons, he discovered the lush meadows and riparian riverbank areas of the Animas River valley. While abundant rainfall that year made the valley's rich grasslands an appealing location for a ranch, Gray still had a problem; a local outlaw by the name of Curley Bill Brocius claimed the land for his own and extorted a $300 payment from Gray to give him rights to ranch in the area.

In 1881 Gray built a house, and with much enthusiasm set up his operation. His zest for the operation quickly faded, however, when one of his sons died under mysterious circumstances during that same year.

The following year James B. Haggin, an agent for William Randolph Hearst, was buying up small ranches in the area on behalf of the newspaper baron. Gray sold out and the ranch became part of a new, vast cattle operation called the Victoria Land and Cattle Company.

Though Gray departed for Arizona, the property still bears his name. Subsequently, the ranch was split up and sold, with part of the property going to the Phelps-Dodge Corporation that has mining and mineral interests in the area. The old Diamond A brand was kept by another owner, so the Gray now runs under the Arrowhead brand.

A RARE PRESERVE

While still run as a working ranch, the fate of the Gray is in question. Some conservationists insist the region be preserved as a wildlife refuge. Government scientists say few areas in the United States boast such a diversity of mammals, breeding birds, reptiles and plants. Antelope, mule and white-tail deer, black bear, mountain lions, javelina, coatimundi, feral hogs and rattlesnakes flourish here.

Sharing a border with Mexico, the Gray preserves both a fascinating history and Old Mexican traditions, including some of the tastiest south-of-the-border treats that any tired, hungry cowboy could ever want.

Originally a traditional cow-calf operation, in 1980 the Gray switched to running a straight yearling-steer outfit. The Gray employs 12 full-time cowboys, each running more than 1,00 steers at his own cow camp. With names like Timberlake, XT, Upshaw, Godfrey, Adobes, Culberson and Fitzpatrick, the camps perpetuate the names of the small ranches that were purchased to make up the present Gray. All the camps have phones, so Lonnie Moore can assure the ranch runs smoothly without having to drive all over southwestern New Mexico. Like a small ranch within the larger ranch, each cow camp operates autonomously to contribute to the whole.

Young mixed-breed steers are shipped up from Mexico, where the former ranch owner Pablo Brener lives. Brener owns meat packing plants south of the border from where he ships his steers for fattening at the ranch for 90 to 120 days.

Branded and doctored by the Gray's cowboys, the steers are turned onto the rich Gray Ranch grasses at individual camps, where they fatten, gaining more than a pound and a half a day. Finally rounded up and loaded onto semi trucks, the steers are shipped to Texas feedlots. In about a month, a new load of young steers arrives and the process starts all over again.

THE LONELINESS OF THE RANGE

The open expanses of the Gray require the most of cowboys. The work is hard, and many cowpokes bring their wives along to work side-by-side with them. Recently ten out of 12 hands at the Gray were married.

Isolation at the Gray means the cowboys must be alone for long periods, but punchers develop a tolerance for being alone and even favor the wild openness of these rugged lands. A cowboy who wants to go to town every night to socialize will find the Gray a difficult place to work.

Cattle drive on the Gray Ranch south of Animas, New Mexico.

The Gray Ranch typifies the larger Western ranches far from any town or city; cowboys learn to do for themselves. There's no vet out here to doctor the animals and there's no M.D., either, to see to human medical needs. We even know of incidents throughout the West where a cowboy broke a leg or an arm out on the range and without complaint set the bone himself. Cowboys speak of these situations rarely if at all. Talking about responding to the extraordinary demands of cowboy life might be perceived by others as bragging, a weakness that warrants taciturn stares and disapproval from the other cowboys. Without companionship save for immediate family, wives find life out here hard too, though there are advantages to working here. Pay starts at $750 a month. The ranch provides groceries, a beef, a house and horses. Because each cowboy runs his own place, everyone at the Gray feels a sense of independence.

Lonnie Moore reminds anyone within earshot that at his ranch he hires only good cowboys and not buckaroos. Like many cowboys, Lonnie disdains the buckaroo who likes to think he is descended from the Spanish Southwest vaquero. With his stampede strings on his hat and his extra-long braided rawhide rope, a buckaroo, in Lonnie's estimate, may feature himself a member of the most elite group of cowboys, but in truth may come up short in horse sense.

OFF THE BACK OF A HORSE

"I've never seen one who could handle a horse." Lonnie winks and smiles. "They ride rough horses, use snaffle bits and they go for one of them runnin' buckin' rides each morning. They use 60-foot ropes all hanging out there. We use 30-foot ropes and we dally. You need a better horse for that."
The cowboys out here work all day on horseback. The Gray Ranch is one of the few outfits that still takes out the ranch wagon each fall during roundup so the cowboys can make a camp. The wagons carry all their gear and food, similar to the old chuck and gear wagons of the trail drive days.

On most smaller modern operations, cowboys drive pickups and horse trailers to the day's worksite and return late each night after providing temporary holding pens for the cattle.

On the vast Gray Ranch, cowboys round up the herd and drive them from horseback, just as in the old days, and they carry all their necessities with them in their mobile ranch wagon.

Horses still provide a crucial element in all aspects of ranch work at the Gray. The outfit owns mostly American quarter horses—70 saddle horses, 32 brood mares and three stallions, to be exact. "We usually have over 100 saddle horses, but our horses got old, so we have a lot of will-bes and has-beens," Lonnie laughs.

Water has always been a precious commodity on arid Western ranches. The Gray operates more than 70 windmills. The ranch hires one man, a windmiller, who does nothing day in and day out except keep the windmills in operating condition. Winter creek water and water collected in large earthen tanks after spring runoff and rains supplement what the windmills pump. The ranch has range enough for the grasslands to be preserved year-round and water enough for the cattle and wildlife to thrive and fatten. The Gray range is always in top-notch condition.

Lonnie's wife Mary comes from the Playas Valley east of the Animas Mountains where her parents still ranch. She enjoys sharing cooking duties with her daughter-in-law, Danielle, who is married to one of the Moores' two sons, Richard. Like his younger brother David, Richard cowboys at the ranch. Both of Danielle's grandfathers cowboyed in the area, and her father was a champion rodeo team roper.

Mary and Danielle often turn out meals for hungry crews of twenty cowboys. Mary likes the basics—steak, potatoes, gravy and beans, and she leaves dessert to Danielle. Danielle loves to make Southwestern treats like the local puff bread called sopaipillas which are filled with honey before being eaten. Sopaipillas can satisfy any cowboy's sweet tooth.

Danielle's Sopaipillas

3 packages yeast
1½ cups warm water
6 cups flour
6 tablespoons baking powder
3 tablespoons salt
1½ cups buttermilk
6 tablespoons vegetable oil
vegetable oil for frying

Dissolve the yeast in the warm water.

Sift the flour, baking powder and salt together and mix in the buttermilk and oil. Add the yeast water and mix thoroughly. Let mixture rise for 1 hour and punch down. Roll out to 1/4" thickness, then cut into triangles or squares. Let rise for another hour. Cook 3 or 4 at a time in very hot oil, 1 minute on each side or until light brown. Drain before serving.

Yield 12

CASCABEL LAND & CATTLE COMPANY
ANIMAS, NEW MEXICO

BRANGUS AND STORMS TO REMEMBER
Carolyn Schwickerath, Ace Ranch Cook

Down in the southwest corner of New Mexico, south of the tiny ranching town of Animas, the empty and desolate boot heel country is the most deserted landscape in the state. Miles from main roads and mailboxes, ranch houses nestle in the mountainous desert country where rattlesnakes sun themselves daily on the rocks. Even going to town for provisions can prove an adventure for ranch cooks in the area.

At about 5,400 feet elevation in the foothills of the rugged Peloncillo Mountains that run along the New Mexico-Arizona border, the Cascabel Land and Cattle Company works 39 sections (25,000 acres) of deeded and Forest Service lease land.

Unlike the vast Gray Ranch, the Cascabel runs for most of the year with only the help of transplanted Iowans Charlie and Carolyn Schwickerath and their four children, with a part-time fencer. Owned by Reese Woodling, cousin of former New York Yankee great Gene Woodling, the Cascabel is a cow/calf outfit. Manager Charlie Schwickerath, who got the job by listing himself with a ranch placement firm, says he thinks of himself more as a cattleman than as a cowboy.

He refers to the fact that a cattleman has to be able to do more than herd, brand and round up cattle. He has to repair all the ranch equipment, run fence, and do many other ranch jobs that require real diversity from the ranchman.

The Cascabel produces some of the choice Brangus in the area, and they sell their breeding stock to many neighboring ranches and operations located throughout the Southwest.

Developed in Louisiana in 1930, Brangus were first bred to capitalize on the superior carcass quality and fertility of Angus cattle and the traveling ability and longevity of Brahman. Many producers say that for the Southwest range country, no breed can beat the Brangus.

Charlie and Carolyn both tend the mother cows and their calves. Bulls are raised on another division of the Cascabel managed by Allan and Carol Crockett over by Benson, Arizona.

Coyotes, mountain lions, deer, javelina and coatimundi, a relative of the raccoon, wander through the ranchlands that are remarkably fertile, considering the lack of rainfall.

When precipitation does come, the rains can cause one heap of trouble. Storms develop rapidly and move with a violence unknown in other areas of the country.

FLASHFLOOD

One day when Charlie, Carolyn, their two daughters and son were returning home from a shopping trip to Douglas, Arizona, located 45 miles away, they encountered a typical desert storm.

Now these storms can be really exciting to watch from a distance, with their brooding

101

clouds, fierce lightning, violent winds and driving rains. To be caught in such a tempest is another matter.

To get to the ranch, the Schwickeraths had to traverse the forbidding Peloncillo Mountains, where few roads go and virtually no one lives. As the storm broke, they found themselves confronted with the prospect of having to cross a mountain stream a number of times. Charlie knew that at some point that stream had to swell with flash-flood waters, possibly stalling their pickup, or worse, engulfing the vehicle and drowning the occupants.

As the rain intensified and the thunder rolled, the Schwickeraths negotiated the stream 15 times before their luck ran out. As they were attempting to cross the stream the 16th time, their four-wheel-drive pickup was swallowed in flash-flood waters that crept ever closer to the car windows.

One by one the family crawled out the window and onto the hood. Charlie could just make out a nearby bank where they could jump to safety before the truck was swept away in the rising flood.

Urging the others on, Charlie and Carolyn made the jump successfully. Each of the Schwickerath girls leaped for the bank and managed to clear the raging waters, until only their son Shane remained. Shane made a desperate lunge, but miscalculated, falling into the torrent, which dragged him under. Charlie reacted quickly to save his son.

"I grabbed him by the back of his coat collar and pulled him out," Charlie says. Drenched and dirty but relieved, the Schwickeraths got back to the Cascabel, leaving the truck to be retrieved after the flood waters subsided.

The next day, when they returned to the site of their adventure, they were saddened to see that all their groceries they had driven so far to buy had been soaked and ruined. But they were happy to be alive.

BRANDING TIME AT THE CASCABEL

From July until early November rattlesnakes pose another hazard, especially in the high desert. Charlie says he had nightmares after he killed his first two rattlers. Now he

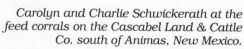

Carolyn and Charlie Schwickerath at the feed corrals on the Cascabel Land & Cattle Co. south of Animas, New Mexico.

travels with his trusty .30-.30 or his .45 caliber pistol loaded and at the ready. For some unknown reason the snakes don't seem to come near the house, says Carolyn with relief.

When they were younger, the Schwickerath kids really enjoyed spring branding and roundup and shipping in the fall because it gave them many opportunities to ride, and they enjoyed working the cattle. Even now, city folks from as far away as Tucson, usually Reese Woodling's friends, come out to the Cascabel to spend a day or two being cowboys. All this amateur help usually creates its share of chaos when the herds stampede or scatter. Though frustrating, the job is made easier because branding is done in chutes and on calf tables requiring few roping skills.

Carolyn cooks for the entire crew as well as the family during these times, but she enjoys her creative expression, preferring to improvise on her recipes by raiding her garden near the house for fresh tomatoes, onions, peppers and jalapeños.

"I like to blend Midwestern fare with a little bit of the Southwest," says this transplanted Midwesterner with a generous smile.

At brandings, when all the guests are gathered around the table, Carolyn serves her apple pie in pans, providing a demonstration of her baking methods that has all the city people scrambling for pens and paper to write down her recipe.

"You have to use Gold Medal flour and Crisco vegetable shortening to really make my pie right," Carolyn says.

Carolyn's Apple Pie

Apple Mixture:
6 to 7 large apples (firm green Golden Delicious
and Jonathans are good), cored, peeled and sliced
1¼ to 1½ cups sugar
¼ cup flour
½ to 1 teaspoon ground cinnamon
Pinch of salt
⅛ cup dark brown sugar
Crust:
3 heaping cups all-purpose Gold Medal Flour
¼ tablespoon salt
1½ cups Crisco shortening
¼ tablespoon margarine, sugar, and cream

Mix together all the ingredients for the filling, coating apples well. Set aside.

Mix the flour and salt together. Cut shortening into flour mixture with a fork until mixture is an evenly crumbled texture. Don't overmix at this point. Using a serving tablespoon, add 15 to 17 spoons of cold water. Mix thoroughly but not too long. Crust will be tough if overmixed after water is added. Divide in two parts.

Roll out onto a floured board, using one part for the bottom crust and one for the top crust. Gently press bottom crust into 9" pie pan.

Spread the apple mixture evenly in the pan. Dot margarine over top of apple mixture. Roll out top crust and place over pie. Baste the top with cream and sprinkle sugar over pie. Cut slits. Crimp the edges to seal it.

Bake at 400 degrees F. for 20 minutes, reduce the heat, and then bake at 350 degrees F. for 55 minutes.

FLYING LAZY S PINTO RANCH
CHINO VALLEY, ARIZONA

HOME OF THE MONTANA KID

Ace Brannaman, Owner/Operator, Man of Many Names & Cook

Most everyone in south-central Arizona has heard of Ace Brannaman. We first met Ace when we were visiting friends in Payson. They invited us to go on a ride along the old Camp Verde freight wagon train route. Ace rode a high-stepping pinto pony adorned with a silver-mounted parade saddle and bridle he had built himself.

At lunch he entertained the crowd by having his horse perform tricks while he told stories about the Old West. He was 74 then and he's 91 now, and still performing and telling yarns.

By big outfit standards, Ace doesn't own much of a ranch; he has about ten acres and a mobile home at the end of Morgan Trail Road about eight miles west of the little town of Chino Valley in the heart of cactus, sagebrush and lava rock country.
But his fences are good and he keeps the yard neat. His two beloved pintos have complete run of the place.

SHIBLAYINE

Ace sent his partner, Lil, out to meet us so we wouldn't get lost, because the road takes a lot of twists and turns before a visitor gets to the ranch. A large sign greeted us when we arrived at his outfit—"WARNING, From the Flying Lazy S Pinto Ranch," the sign said. "All Cowboys and Cowgirls Who Ride Past and Don't Stop For Chow Will Be Shot or Hung As I Don't Have Time To Call The Sheriff. Signed, The Montana Kid."

Those words tell a lot about Ace. He's pure quill cowboy and nobody forgets him because he captures the past as a living symbol of the Old West. He's also a walking history book. Ace calls himself the Montana Kid. His likeness was the trick roping cowboy who once graced Kellogg's Corn Flakes boxes. Ace came by his name in a rather interesting fashion.

"My given name is Shiblayine," he says. "It's Cheyenne and means Little White Horse." Born in Montana in 1911, he first started school near Bozeman. The other students couldn't pronounce Shiblayine, so the kids started calling him Ace, and the name stuck.

Ace grew up cowboying and later became a rodeo bronc rider, a horse trainer, a saddle and boot maker, a game warden, a veterinarian, a trick roper and Hollywood stunt man. As the Montana Kid, he still travels around with his two pinto ponies and his constant companion Lillian, putting on shows at senior citizens' centers, schools and youth hospitals.

"I love kids," he says. "And I know kids love cowboys. When I was a kid, all I ever wanted was a red silk neck rag and a big black hat."

BRONCO WILLIE BRANNAMAN

Ace's father, a full-blooded Cheyenne Indian named Bronco Willie, bought cattle for Swift Packing Company. He also was a rodeo cowboy, horse trainer and trick roper. Ace says his father's parents were killed in the battle of the Little Big Horn when Bronco Willie was five years old.

"Bronco Willie and his orphaned brother were taken in by a friendly rancher named Brannaman who lived way out in the country south of Bozeman.

"Brannaman kept them two boys hidden in his basement until they were ten years old and took them out only at night so's no one would see 'em. He taught them boys to hunt and fish and ride horses. When they got older, Brannaman gave them his name and taught 'em how to make a living in the white man's world.

"I've seen a lot of history in my time, and while I may tell a lie here and there, you better believe me, because I was the only one there," he says.

His mother's grandfather, Fred Smith, was a saddle and boot maker in St. Louis. Smith and his brother argued over wages with the shop owner, and to settle the differences, the Smith boys left town with a wheelbarrow full of company tools.

"They took out across the plains pushing that wheelbarrow until they came to an Indian village. They tooled scenes of the Indians and their horses into leather and gave it to the chiefs. The Indians thought the leather workers possessed powerful spirits and treated them like gods. The chiefs had the braves push the wheelbarrow to the next village, and in this manner Grandpa Smith made it across the plains to Bozeman, Montana."

Mounted on the wall of his

Ace Brannaman, the Montana Kid at the Flying Lazy S Pinto Ranch.

106

home, Ace has an old .31-caliber Lancaster rifle. He says his Grandfather Smith had that piece on his trip across the prairie. Ace never will sell that rifle, one of the last made by Lancaster.

A Pair of Boots for the James Boys

Grandpa Smith once made new boots for the outlaws Frank and Jesse James, Ace says. "They robbed a bank in Minnesota and came to Bozeman to lay low for awhile. Grandpa built them some boots and they stayed with him all the while. While the outlaws waited at Grandpa's shop, the local bank was in the process of foreclosing on a neighboring widow's ranch."

Frank and Jesse decided to intervene, according to Ace. Frank went out to the widow's home and gave her money to pay the bankers who showed up later to collect their payment. When the bankers left the ranch, Jesse robbed them and took the money back.

Ace learned saddle and boot making from his grandfather and still practices these trades. "I've built over a thousand saddles, and I don't even have one of my own to sit in. Before I die I want to ride in one of my own saddles."

Ace said his father, Bronco Willie, became a pretty fair bucking horse rider while traveling around buying beef for Swift and Company. He often entered rodeos in towns where he stayed with his family.

Before Ace was ten years old, he too entered the action, riding some of the same stock from which Bronco Willie had just been bucked. At age twelve, Ace rode in the famous old Prescott rodeo and made it to the money. A faded old photograph shows the young cowboy seated on a high-snapping bronc in old-time Prescott.

"My dad never treated me like a kid," he says. "If I wanted to do something, he'd always say, `Go for it.' I raised my own boys the same way."

An Old Showman

Ace has one son who is confined to a hospital due to chronic illness, but his other boy, Buckshot, is an accomplished horse trainer, and magazine ads featuring Western wear frequently show him modeling cowboys hats, shirts and other paraphernalia.

When the two Brannaman boys were young, Ace taught them to rope and ride. Like his father before him, Ace took his family on the road. The Brannamans did well for many years, performing at rodeos and fairs and putting on shows in hospitals and youth homes.

An eyecatching trio with their black and white horses, red silk neck rags, big black hats and limber ropes, the Brannamans performed in television and radio commercials and signed on as reps for Kellogg's Corn Flakes. When the oldest boy became ill, his mother pulled him off the road, and that, Ace says, ended the trio and their marriage.

Today, Lil is Ace's new partner, and they still like to hit the road every so often. Even if they don't travel as far as they did in the old days, they still please the crowds. Offspring of his original horses, his two pintos play dead, count, dance, and even undress Ace, push him around, and in general, steal the show from the old master showman.

Ace's love for horses runs deep. Raised on a ranch with horses all his life, Ace has also studied animal health. After a stay in Alaska as a game warden, Ace became a veterinarian.

"I went to Alaska back in 1931. There were only two thousand people in Anchorage at the time. I got a job as a federal game warden and was paid $28.00 a month and had a house provided."

The government hired him after he became a vet to study results of radiation on animals in the Pacific islands during atomic bomb testing. He gave up veterinary medicine because he felt confined and he wanted to be outdoors more. Cowboys love to roam and see what's over the next ridge. From their home, Ace and Lil ride to visit ruins of an Indian tribe that lived near their ranch centuries ago and vanished without a trace.

Ace is also a first-order ranch cook and a most hospitable host. Visitors in his home know they're in the real West talking to a real cowboy. He does most of the talking and pretty near all the cooking. Lil listens and smiles.

Many cowboy cooks swear by sourdough. They say that good sourdough is the mark of a real ranch cook. Ace's sourdough starter is over a hundred years old and has been passed down from cowboy cook to cowboy cook.

AUTHOR'S NOTE: Since this interview, Ace Brannaman has passed away.

Montana Kid Sourdough Pancakes

1 cup sourdough starter

½ cup water

3 tablespoons sugar

1 to 1½ cups flour

3 tablespoons vegetable oil

1 egg

Place sourdough starter in bowl. Add water, sugar, and enough flour to make a loose batter. Let mixture sit for 10 minutes or more until it starts to bubble.

Add the oil and egg. Spoon onto a hot greased griddle and cook until done, turning once.

Ace's Sourdough Biscuits

For biscuits, just make the pancake mix a bit stiffer so you can roll it out.
Preheat the oven to 350 degrees F. and grease your biscuit pan. Pinch off small fistfuls of dough and put 'em in pan. Pop 'em in the oven and brown 'em good.

AV BAR RANCH
KLONDYKE, ARIZONA

WHERE COWBOYS STILL HITCH THEIR HORSES TO THE FRONT PORCH RAIL
Jim "J.R." Robinson, Bronc Rider, Cowboy, Cook

We met Jim Robinson through Tom's ex-wife Nancy, a wilderness guard for three years in Idaho's Selway-Bitterroot Wilderness. Everyone up there called him "J.R." and he became a guide for a big game hunting camp near Fish Lake, where Nancy lived alone in a cabin.

J.R. had originally hired on as a cook with the outfitter, but after the boss fired one of the guides, he brought Jim aboard. A beat-up old cowboy, J.R. tried his damnedest to be a good guide, but an old war wound made the rigors of climbing up and down the steep, wet slopes of the Selway trying for Jim. He decided to leave for warmer climes in Arizona.

Tom and Nancy met up with J.R. on the AV Bar Ranch, 28 miles up a dirt road from Pima, over in the state's southeast corner directly north of Willcox, the home of the old singing cowboy himself, Rex Allen.

Located in the Aravaipa Canyon near the Coronado National Forest right close to the town of Klondyke, the AV Bar features sprawling stands of cottonwoods that grow along a creek where the trees shelter the white, wood-frame ranch house. Out back, a vehicle shop, a hay shed and a horse corral built of mesquite tree trunks and twisted wire serve the ranch.

Klondyke consists of little more than a general store-post office where mail deliveries happen twice a week. Cowboys still ride up and tie tired horses to the front porch hitch rail.

In 1918, a fight between the Power boys and the local sheriff broke out near the store. Accused of draft dodging, the Powers were living in a cabin in the nearby Galiuro Mountains, now know as the Galiuro Wilderness, where the actual shootout took place.

According to store manager Ed Robinette, the lawman shot and killed the elder Power at the cabin. One of the boys, Tom Power, escaped, but was later captured and spent 40 years in the state prison, and wrote a book entitled *Shootout at Dawn, an Arizona Tragedy*. For those interested in learning more about the confrontation, Robinette said the book should be available through your local bookstore, or you can order it from him at (602) 828-3386.

TOUGH AS WANG LEATHER

When we arrived, J.R. was working as the only cowboy on the ranch, caring for a small herd of Hereford cattle and a few good saddle horses. On short notice with the management, J.R. left not long after we did. We never did meet the owner, Gordon Whiting, but understand he owns several southern Arizona ranches. Cattle fatten on the AV Bar before being shipped to feedlots or to another one of Whiting's ranches.

Tough as wang leather and independent as a barn cat, Jim Robinson is one-hundred-percent cowboy. In his woolen vest, silk neck rag, Western hat with Montana crease and high-top boots with four-inch heels, Jim walks with a limp like many an old-time cowboy. J.R.'s taken hard falls from many bad broncs, and has had his back broken, as well as several other bones.

In 1970 he worked on an outfit near Deeth, Nevada. A colt ran him into a fence, resulting in a pretty bad wreck. "This colt was six years old and hadn't seen a man in three years. I promised myself I'd quit riding bucking horses, but the foreman said, `Oh, you're supposed to be a big, bad, bronc rider.' So I got on the son-of-a-bitch and he bucked through three lodgepole corral fences. He hooked my foot on a post and twisted my back. I heard something pop."

The newspaper account of Jim's wreck reported that J.R. had dislocated a disc, ruptured another, cracked six ribs and moved two more. He had a blood clot on his spinal column. The doctors told him he'd be lucky to walk. And he would never ride a horse again.

But cowboys hardly ever quit on a sawbones' say-so and J.R. was soon back in the saddle.

"My back bothers the hell out of me," he says. "Shoeing just about kills me and I can't stand up straight on cold, wet days." While we visited J.R., he had to move some cattle and shoe a horse. We watched as he trimmed one foot, limped around awhile, trimmed another foot and limped around some more, clearly in great pain.

He tied the horse to a hitch rack near the tack room and kept his tools and anvil inside the building. He had to walk back and forth between the horse and the shed to give his back a chance to straighten.

A SURE-ENOUGH BRONC RIDER

"You know what this is?" he asked, as he saddled the 16-hand, 1,250-pound Appaloosa gelding. "This here's a B.D.A.—Big Dumb Appaloosa. You know what they say about Appaloosas? `No tail, no mane, no brain.' You know why the war chiefs made braves ride Appaloosas? `Cause them dumb horses would make the Indians so mad they'd fight anybody."

Tightening the cinch on his Nevada Slick Fork, J.R. bounced up in the saddle, stuck the Mexican rowels into his Appy's flanks and blasted out of the yard in a shower of rocks and gravel. As he topped the ridge by the horse corral, we noticed his straight back and firm seat in the saddle.

They say about old-time bronc busters, "He may walk with a limp, but he sure as hell don't ride with one." Jim Robinson fits that description to a T.

Born in St. Charles County near St. Louis, Missouri in 1937, Jim and his family moved to a ranch near Terry, Montana when he was young. He doesn't recall the Montana move, but remembers growing up on a ranch and riding horses before he could walk, roping wild cattle and breaking wild horses for fun and profit while he attended school.

He even recalls riding a bucking horse when he was about age four.

"We was moving cows and I was riding this big old dumb horse. He started bucking and I started screaming, `This horse is bucking.'

My Pa said, `He ain't bucking; he's just moving rough. Stay on and ride.'"

Such early experiences made a lasting impression on the young J.R.. He grew up riding bucking horses and liking it. And while he rodeoed for a while, he doesn't believe in riding bulls.

"Bulls are for breeding," he said. "It ain't natural for a man to be trying to ride a bull. Horses were made to be rode; that's a natural thing to do and the fun thing to do."

J.R. got to thinking he was a pretty good bronc rider while in high school. He dropped out in tenth grade and went a-rodeoing. He admits that he was probably a typical young, restless cowboy, searching for a dream but never realizing he had already found paradise in ranching, riding and roping at home.

HOLLYWOOD DAYS AND HARD COMBAT

J.R.

ended up in Hollywood, California doing odd jobs, when he got an offer to be in the movies. Jim worked as the attack target for the dog Hero, a stand-in for Rin Tin Tin.

J.R. liked his Hollywood life and went on to become a stunt man, and later trained dogs used in films. Currently, Jim owns a very large, well-trained German shepherd called Hawkeye. Trained as an attack dog, Hawkeye also performs stunts, such as jumping from an airplane in a parachute. Hawkeye watches the ranch with one of his keen eyes open at all times. The other eye stays trained on J.R. The dog never makes a move unless Jim gives the OK.

In 1958 J.R. entered the army, and says that after "swamp training," the military sent him to Laos as an advisor. Shot three times and knifed four times, Jim's body bears testimony to his hard-fought Southeast Asian experience.

After the army, J.R. returned to his first love, cowboying. Like most single hands, he's moved around a lot just to see some country. And like most cowboys, he'll quit his job, roll up his bedroll and go down the road for little or no reason.

"I had this one dumb foreman who was a former irrigator and fence fixer. He knew that a ditch would turn water and a fence would turn a cow, but that's all he knew. I wore my spurs into the kitchen one morning and he told me to take 'em off.

"I said, `Mister, I only dress once a day and I'm already dressed today.' I just quit right there on the spot."

J.R. has worked in almost every state in the far West, as

Jim Robinson and Hawkeye at the AV Bar Ranch.

well as doing a short stint in Florida. He says cattle and horses are about the same every-where you go, but the way cowboys work them differs in almost every state.

"In Arizona, because much of the country is steep and brushy, cowboys tie their ropes hard and fast to the saddle horn, as there is not much time to rope a critter and take a dally. In the open desert country of Oregon and Nevada, cowboys are called buckaroos and use sixty-foot ropes. They have plenty of time to rope a critter, take a dally and stop the critter slowly, playing it like a big fish on a long line."

And like most bachelor cowboys we met on those lonesome, far-away jobs at ranches with strange-sounding names, J.R. has married and divorced—five times. Jim compares women to badgers, saying once they start digging, they don't know when to stop.

He says he enjoys living by himself, and anyway Hawkeye keeps him company. And he has his guitar. An accomplished musician, he says that his whole family played some type of musical instrument. He started on a harmonica at age four and has played in country-western bands to support himself between cowboying jobs.

To J.R., cooking has to be simple, because he's out riding for long hours most every day. When he has time, however, he likes to experiment in the kitchen. Like most every-thing Jim does, sometimes his recipes show a bit of fire.

Here's J.R.'s Cowboy's Experimental Dip. "Be careful not to get it too hot," he grins. "This stuff will blow your socks off!"

J.R.'s Cowboy Experimental Dip

2 1-pound containers sour cream
½ cup good grade picante sauce
a splash of hot sauce
¼ cup hot, coarse horseradish
½ cup diced, mashed sweet onion
¼ cup diced, mashed pitted olives

Blend all the ingredients and taste as you proceed, taking care not to get this mixture too hot for you and your guests. Flavor to taste.

Great with chips, on celery, or as a salad topping or side dish.

Yield: 4½ cups

EUREKA SPRINGS RANCH
BONITA, ARIZONA

A DESERT OASIS
Kim Lackner, Critter Nurse and Cook

A large corporate operation, the Eureka Springs Ranch encompasses 137 sections of prime cattle country in southeastern Arizona. Made of thick adobe, the old ranch buildings were erected in 1880, no doubt providing protection from the hot summer sun and also from menacing Apache Indians.

Jim Robinson at the nearby AV Bar Ranch told us about Eureka Springs. So we drove down the narrow, sandy road through mesquite trees and bunch grass, and were greeted at the entrance gate by obstinate Brangus cattle lying in front of the cattle guard.

Across a dry wash, through very large, old cottonwoods, the white walls of Eureka Springs headquarters glowed, making the ranch appear as an oasis in the desert.

In a land where water holes are few and far between, Eureka Springs provides a sanctuary for man and beast alike. For centuries, desert animals, Indians, wild horses, cattle and weary travelers have come here to slake their thirst.

The Spanish explorer Coronado came through this region, now Graham County, and probably rested and refreshed his men and livestock here.

DESERT DOGS AND ORPHAN HORSES

Named 1986 Arizona Ranch Manager of the year by the Society for Range Management, Don Lackner runs Eureka Springs. Don grew up on a ranch just down the road from Eureka Springs, and is married to Kim, his childhood sweetheart.

Kim met us at ranch headquarters on her way back from the barn, where she doctored a calf that had had its tail pulled off by coyotes. She said she takes in all bum calves, orphaned horses and sick chickens.

Coyotes, ever-present throughout ranching country, cause their share of problems all year, but especially during calving season. The desert dogs run down newborn calves. If the coyotes don't kill a youngster, often they will do severe damage.

"We have five calves in the barn right now with their tails about pulled out," Kim said.

Kim says she remembers her childhood days on a ranch owned by Don's aunt. She loved running out to a bridge or creek crossing after a rain and watching a wall of water rush down the stream bed after a flash flood. Raised in the little town of Pima, about 40 miles to the east, she spent every day she could at the ranch. "Eureka Springs used to be a horse outfit," Kim says. "When we came here the range was overgrazed, the fences were in bad need of repair and the cattle were doing poorly." Don started managing Eureka Springs in 1977. Since then he has slowly improved the buildings, fences and livestock.

Shortly after he arrived, Don sold the excess horses and older cattle and worked with the Forest Service to rest part of the range and develop springs and water traps throughout the ranch. "Lack of water is a big problem in this country and we have put in a lot of dirt dams to trap and hold water," Don says. He also introduced Brangus bulls into his herd and feels that this breed gives him a good range-hardy cross that's disease resistant and fairly easy to handle.

Don's identical twin brother Dan also works on the ranch as expert mechanic and heavy equipment operator, building roads and dams. Dams are important in the desert country.

Rain usually comes in the desert much too fast. Weather and road conditions concern Kim, who does her shopping in Safford, a round trip of over 100 miles, mostly on dirt roads.

With a century-old general store and post office, Bonita, about five miles down the road, doesn't have the groceries needed to sustain a working ranch.

So off Kim goes to Safford once a month, in good weather or bad. "Once in a while I'll get trapped in town and have to stay overnight with Mother," Kim says. "But if there is any way I can make it (back to the ranch), I'll do it."

Kim gets up at four in the morning seven days a week and hasn't had a vacation.. ever. But the peace and beauty of the Springs quietly filters into one's life there, no matter how difficult it may seem to the uninitiated.

JUST GOOD OLD USING HORSES

"We started out trying to raise our own colts," Kim says. "But the stallion was hard on fences and always fought with other horses. It takes five years feeding a colt before you can get a lot of use out of it. We just think it works better for us to buy good geldings about three or four (years old) through auctions." Don trains and shoes all his own horses and he buys most replacement horses needed by the ranch. Most of the ranch work is done a-horseback.

"We like just good old using horses," Kim says. "We like to take young horses and turn 'em loose around here and let 'em develop a rock foot; a nice small foot with a high frog, one that will hold up in all this rock and cactus. You have to have a rock horse to get around in this country."

Don leaves the bulls in with the cows year-round; however, most calves are born in spring as is nature's way. Don brings first-calf heifers down to a calving pasture near headquarters where they are checked daily. Heavy heifers, about to give birth, are brought down near the barn and watched closer than the others.

The Lackners say that because of their Brahma heritage, Brangus cattle are a little mean, so they leave the bulls alone as much as possible.

"With so much country to cover and so many bad-tempered bulls out there, it's just easier to leave 'em in with the cows than it is to try to gather 'em up. We've got one pasture that is over forty sections (40 square miles) by itself."

Don tags each cow and keeps records on her production. He preg-tests cows every fall and culls out old and unproductive ones. Kim's rewards come mostly in the kitchen, even though she does help out with other ranch chores. In addition to taking care of the orphaned and sick critters on the ranch, Kim keeps the books, rides and checks windmills and stock tanks, and cooks for the crew.

GRANDMA'S COOKING

Kim wanted to learn how to cook from her grandmother, with whom she spent much of her time as a child. But her grandmother said that it was easier to do it herself than to supervise a greenhorn kid.

"But when I watched Grandma cook, I used to think, `Boy, she's good.' I've had to teach myself, and I think I'm a better cook for it. I went back and studied Grandmother's methods and her cookbooks. I was determined to learn, and I did, and I'm proud of my cooking."

The ranch, owned by Anderson Development Company, keeps a crew of five hands year-round, and Kim cooks for them as well as the large roundup and branding crews in spring and fall. "We don't hire a lot of outside help," she said. "At roundup and brandings the neighbors pitch in, and we have lots of friends and relatives who come out. Neighbors are good to help out in this country. They help us and we help them."

Neighbors helping neighbors—that's the Eureka Springs way; Dan helps Don, Kim helps the orphaned and busted-up critters.. .and the bulls help themselves. Truly an oasis in this hard desert country, Eureka Springs shines like a diamond.

Kim's Cowboy Steak

¼ cup grated parmesan cheese

salt and pepper

4 steaks of your choice

2 tablespoons bacon grease

1 10½-ounce can mushroom soup

1 cup water

1 small onion, chopped

1 bell pepper, stem and seeds removed, chopped

Mix together the parmesan cheese, salt and pepper. Roll the steaks in this mixture and fry in hot bacon grease, browning both sides.

Mix the soup, water, onion, and bell pepper. Lay the steaks on a cookie sheet and cover with the soup mixture.

Place in a 400-degree oven until the dish forms a crust.

Serves: 4

Kim Lackner at the Eureka Springs Ranch.

THUNDERBIRD RANCH
RIMROCK, ARIZONA

ROUGHEST CATTLE COUNTRY IN THE U.S.
Hilda Sullivan, Rancher, Cowgirl, Cook

Glenn and Ann Everett of Camp Verde told us to talk to Hilda Sullivan. Now retired, Glenn worked as a young man on ranches where Hilda cooked. He says she was one of the best ranch cooks he's ever known. Also retired, she lives in a comfortable house near the little town of Rimrock, just off I-17, about fifty miles south of Flagstaff.

Glenn and Ann took us out to dinner, and after much coffee and talk late in the evening drizzling rain, we shook hands and said good bye. "You go see Hilda," Glenn advised. "You won't be disappointed."

Glenn was right; Hilda Sullivan was wonderful. To be truthful, we never got to visit the Thunderbird Ranch, but we did get to spend an unforgettable evening with former ranch manager, cowgirl and cook, Hilda Sullivan.

While driving up to Rimrock we recalled a story about Arizona that retired State Livestock Inspector Port Parker of Sedona had told us.

Years ago, a California cowboy rode over to visit a rancher friend in Arizona to look over some new country and inquire about employment in the area. After riding the range for a week or so, the two friends stopped one afternoon to look out across the vistas and rest their horses.

The visitor pushed his hat back on his head and squinted his eyes. "You know," he said. "I've traveled a lot of places, but in Arizona I've seen more country and less grass, more rivers and less water and more mountains and fewer trees than I ever seen in my entire life."

SAMMY HAD A ROCK FOOT

To be sure, in Arizona water is scarce, grass is scattered and trees, such as they are, are likely to be covered with thistles and thorns. Cowboys entering the state from other parts of the country have to learn a whole new way of riding, roping and working cattle. Because of the dense brush and rugged country, cattle tend to be wild and hard to gather, and cowboys and cowgirls have to be more hardy than average, abandoning concern for personal safety. Even horses in the Grand Canyon state have to be a little different to work this country. Because of the rock-strewn streambeds, hills and gullies, cowboys want a horse with what they call a rock foot, that is, a small, narrow foot, much like a mule's hoof.

Inspector Parker cowboyed as a youth in the Bradshaw Mountains and said the best horse he ever owned (and he's owned plenty) was a little cold-blooded mustang he called Sammy.

"Sammy was a coon-footed horse (small, flat feet) and had a head as ugly as a hammer. But he would go anywhere. He was the best horse I ever had."

Near the little cowtown of Wagner, Sammy ran off with a bunch of wild horses and

Port never saw him again. However, Port did see that the saddles available in the early 1900s weren't made for the country he had to work.

In 1933 he worked with Porter Saddlery in Phoenix and they built "The Port Parker Saddle," a new design with good swells and a moderately high cantle still emulated and used today.

The mountainous, brushy country where Port cowboyed has been called by *Western Horseman Magazine* the roughest cattle country in the United States, a jungle of manzanita bushes and thorny chaparrals laced with rocky ridges and sheer ledges that tend to intimidate even the boldest of cowboys.

In Arizona they say there are old cowboys and there are bold cowboys, but there are no old, bold cowboys.

In the 15th and 16th centuries cattle escaped from Spanish explorers in Arizona, propagated, and grew wilder with each generation.

Fond of Arizona, prolific Western author Zane Grey owned a cabin at the base of the Mogollon Rim near Payson, not too far east of Rimrock. There he wrote many of his cattle-ranching novels detailing all the accoutrements of cowboying. Grey particularly liked to ride the open Arizona countryside and observe firsthand the trails and water holes, and the types of people and horses which he so vividly portrayed in his books.

In 1914 Hilda Bruce Sullivan came into this Zane Grey country, the first of four children born near Montezuma Castle, now a national monument close to Rimrock. Her father, Earl Bruce, homesteaded a ranch there.

Being the oldest, Hilda became her father's helper. Being a girl didn't mean she worked any less.

"I caught a lot of men's work from my Dad. He was an honest-to-God cowman. He used a sixty-foot rope and he didn't throw it very often, but when he did, now there would be something on the end of it. We worked cattle most every day and I sure did my part of the work."

As her father's cowhand, Hilda never learned to cook until later in life.

"Things were tough in them days before the war (WW II). I mean, you almost had to buy a job to get one. I was working as a kitchen helper on a ranch during fall roundup and another outfit sent a rep over to hire me to cook. I didn't really want to go, but times were hard and cooking meant more money, so I went."

The new outfit hauled Hilda out in the countryside south of Happy Jack and dumped her off to cook for their roundup.

"That place was just a set of corrals out there in the brush and they put me up in a little tent and said, 'Go to it, girl.' They had a wood stove for me to cook on, but it got the tent so hot I couldn't stand it. I did all my cooking outside on the ground in a Dutch oven. It rained, and things were muddy and sloppy, just a hell'va mess, but I kept them cowboys filled up with beans and steaks and lots of hot coffee."

Since that auspicious beginning, Hilda has cooked and cowboyed on many ranches. She even managed a ranch for several years.

"Now that was a freak thing," she says. "After my folks retired, they sold their ranch and moved into town. I was cooking on a real big ranch and the foreman told me he had heard of an outfit that needed a manager and he had recommended me. I couldn't believe it."

The foreman told Hilda he had considered every hand he knew of and he believed her to be the best person for the job.

"Life sure deals you some funny cards," she says. "Sometimes they may come off the bottom of the deck but you have to play 'em the way they come to you."

The outfit where Hilda had received her opening turned out to be her father's old homestead, the Thunderbird Ranch.

COYOTE AROUND AND TALK SWEET

At the time of the manager's job offer, Hilda's husband Joe worked for the Forest Service and she felt uncertain how he might react to her new position. "We talked it over and he said, `Why sure. You can do it as well as anyone can.' So I took the job in 1953 and I ran that ranch for over nine years."

When Joe had time off, he helped Hilda. She says the Thunderbird turned out some of the fattest cattle ever to come out of the hills around Montezuma.

"I work cattle slow and easy," she says. "I learned that from my dad. Just coyote around and talk sweet. That's the way to handle cattle. Nervous cattle don't gain well. A shook-up critter will shrink in a hurry. Joe and I never did much roping, only when we absolutely had to.

"A good dog is indispensable in working cattle in the brush and a good horse is an absolute necessity. Ain't much of a ranch without a couple of good horses. I never want to get away from horses and cattle."

Life has dealt Hilda some bad hands, too. In his later years, Joe suffered a stroke and Hilda had to put him in a care facility.

"I moved into town in a little apartment to be near him," she says. "It was so unnatural to me, I just about went crazy. But you do what you have to do. I'd go to the mirror and look right in my eyes and say, `Now this has been dealt to you, so you play it and make the best of it.'"

To save her sanity, the range rider from Rimrock turned to what she knew best.

"I started training horses for other people," she says. "I'd been around horses all my life and knew what made a good horse. Pretty soon I had more horses to train than I could handle. I'm about getting too old for that now, but I still love getting up on a good horse."

THE BEAUTY OF BEANS

The world has changed since the days when she rode a pony back and forth seven miles to school as a youngster. "I saw the end of the open range," Hilda says. "I saw the last of the big drives and the first cattle truck that ever came into this country. I saw outfits go from horse-drawn chuck wagons to chuck trailers pulled by pickups, to motor-driven kitchens. I've seen the wire put up and the invasion of the three-wheelers. I've seen good ranches turned into golf courses. They call that progress. I'd rather not say what I call it."

The abilities of a good cowboy haven't changed, though. "A good cowman has got to out-think a cow," she says. "He's got to be part cow and part horse. A real, honest-to-God working cowboy today is a rare find. By God, if you see a cowboy this day in time, stop and stare, you're looking at a real antique."

Hilda also points out the practicality of continuing to cook on her old wood stove that she has hung on to all these years. "I prefer a wood stove for cooking. It heats the house and the food and it keeps the cook warm. That's a hell'va good deal." While she doesn't cook outdoors much any more, Hilda still has a reputation in the Verde Valley as one of the best cooks ever. One old-time cowboy in Camp Verde told us, "Yep, Hilda Sullivan fed a lot of hands in her time. She's what you call a gore-may cook, a real good 'un."

Hilda retorts, "I ain't never been a gourmet cook. They dirty too many dishes and that ain't my style. And I ain't never been much for recipes. That's too much trouble. I just throw things together, a little of this and a little of that, but the cowboys love it.

"To make a real good cowboy supper, you need steak and beans. Beans can be reheated and re-served many times, and they seem to get better with each reheating. That's the beauty of beans. I love steak and beans about as much as I love ranching, and ranching was bred in me; it's in my blood, especially cowboy cooking. It was my way of life."

Hilda's Round Steak

Take a good-quality round steak and tenderize it real good on both sides; criss-cross it with a butcher knife and really whack it.

Roll it in flour, salt and pepper and cook in a slightly greased pan. After the steaks are done, mix flour and milk in the pan and make a delicious gravy.

Hilda's Cowboy Cooking Pinto Beans

2 cups dried pinto beans
1 tablespoon bacon grease
1 clove garlic, minced
½ cup chopped green chile
½ cup catsup
1 teaspoon Worcestershire sauce

Completely cover beans with water and soak at least overnight. (Soaking for 24 hours is better.) Beans may be cooked in soaking water. Add the bacon fat to the water to keep from boiling over. Add the garlic and green chile peppers.

Add the catsup and Worcestershire sauce.

Cook with a tight lid (the tighter the better) and cook at least eight to 10 hours.

Keep beans covered with water and add hot water if more is needed. Do not salt beans while they're cooking. (Salt seems to keep 'em from cooking through.)

Serves: 4 to 6

RIGDEN RANCH
KIRKLAND, ARIZONA

WHERE LONGHORNS ROAM
Margaret Rigden, Cook

Out in the rolling hills southwest of Prescott, we traveled through the open country of Skull Valley about five miles up a narrow road from Highway 89 to the little town of Kirkland. A quick mile west of town, a short dirt road follows Kirkland Creek to the Rigden Ranch.

Near the century-old, white wood-frame house surrounded by tall elm trees, a goat-proof fence encloses the shady yard. A large, rough-cut lumber barn about a hundred yards east of the home shelters the saddle horses belonging to this old family ranch.

Carrying himself with an air of authority, Tom Rigden met us at his door. Though 75 years old and blind, he still monitors all events that occur on the Rigden spread. The Agricultural Extension Office in Phoenix had informed us that he ranch, one of the finest family outfits in Arizona, might make an interesting visit in our quest for ranch cooks.

Diabetes has taken Tom's sight, but nothing has taken his wit or his knowledge of the country and cattle.

"I don't see too good any more," Tom says, "but I've got a good hand here in Cynthia (his 44-year-old daughter). And a good cook (wife Margaret)—that's all you need to run a ranch."

Tom still rides out to help Cynthia with ranching chores. "I can tell where I am in this country by the feel of the ground under my horse's feet. Our cattle are used to me, so Cynthia positions me where she wants me. I can still turn a cow. They don't know that I can't see 'em."

Born and raised in the old Rigden place, Tom still lives in the house built by his father, who came to Arizona from England as a small boy.

"He was a rough and tough son-of-a-gun," Tom says of his father. "As he worked his way west, he got a job on a ranch in Colorado making $4.00 a month. But at the end of the first month, the owners refused to pay him, because they said he ate more than the ranch could afford."

Once the Angora capital of the world, Skull Valley boasted many goat ranches, but Tom points out that he is not, never has been, and never will be in the goat business.

"Don't even say 'goat' to me," he says. "It's a dirty word." The Rigdens resisted going into goat ranching at a time when most other outfits in the area could hardly wait to get into the goat business. The Rigdens stuck with what they knew best.

"Cattle was and is our way of life," Tom says. "It always will be."

Now responsible for running the ranch, Cynthia has some different ideas from Tom about how to turn a profit in the livestock business.

A HUNDRED TIMES THE VALUE

An accomplished Western artist and sculptor, Cynthia breeds and raises Texas long-horn cattle, not for beef, but to give her models for her art work. "I've made per-haps a hundred times over the market value of a critter just by keeping it around

120

to pose for me," she said. Bronzes of bucking colts, frisky calves, running horses and sleeping cows fill the Rigden yard, house and Cynthia's studio out back. Shown at well-known Western art galleries and shows, her work commands a high price.

Cynthia prefers sculpture, but she also draws and paints, each rendition a perfect study in animal anatomy, proportion and movement.

During our visit Cynthia was breaking a couple of yearling longhorn steers, both for ranch work and to pull a cart for show in parades.

"I need a couple of work oxen to pull loads of hay out to the stock during snowstorms and to pull a fresno to dig ditches and level roadbeds," Cynthia says.

She likes longhorns because they are so adaptive and smart. Once she had a young longhorn mother who, bawling and crying, met her as she rode out to check cattle after a severe flash flood. "This old mamma really put up a fuss. She jumped the creek and ran back up in the brush, just like she was trying to tell me something."

Scouting around, Cynthia found the baby calf upside down, nearly drowned in a wash. "That old cow seemed to know that I could help," Cynthia says.

Cynthia trains her own horses. She takes horses off the race track and turns them into ranch stock.

"We use a lot of thoroughbreds," she says. "Once you get all that foolishness out of them, they settle down and make real good cow horses. They are big and strong and can cover a lot of country, and you still have a horse under you at the end of the day."

In addition to working cattle with thoroughbreds, Cynthia also uses the big horses as models for her art work. "This one old boy has made me more money as a model than he ever did for his owner on the track," she says of a gelding sold to her cheaply, with the understanding that she give him a good home.

Caring for calves, riding fence, training oxen and breaking horses fill Cynthia's week. Then she finishes each long day by working in her studio until around midnight almost every evening.

To compensate for her rigorous schedule, she sleeps in until about eight in the morning, a luxury on a ranch.

Tom still gets up at first light and does morning chores. With his homemade walking stick and two friendly dogs, he completes the job with no trouble. Well, almost no trouble...

Back in '86, as Tom reached in a grain barrel, a rogue ground squirrel bit him on the hand. First, he had to take the series of extremely painful rabies shots, and then the wound became infected. The doctors removed one of his little fingers in order to save the hand.

Another time, Tom almost stepped on a rattlesnake on the way to the barn, but an alert cowboy pulled him out of harm's way at the last instant.

BARRIGA LLENA CORAZON CONTENTO

On the Rigden Ranch, Tom's wife Margaret, as cook, provides the heart and soul of the place. "On any ranch in the world, the cook works harder than anyone else," Tom says. No one works with more love and care than Margaret Rigden when she's in the kitchen.

A sign on the wall of her kitchen proclaims, "Barriga Llena Corazon Contento" — A full belly causes a happy heart. These words sum up her philosophy.

Born Margaret Hays in 1917, she's a direct descendant of Daniel Boone.

"Daniel Boone's daughter married a Hays, and my father was a Hays," she says.

Margaret's grandfather, Upton Hays, freighted on the Santa Fe Trail in the late 1800s. The story goes that Upton Hays once raced a stagecoach on a mule and won by cutting across country.

"They (the Hayses) had that wandering spirit," she says. "It's in their blood, and I guess it always will be."

Although Margaret has never ventured far from Kirkland, she has seen the world come and go through her kitchen. "We've had visitors from all over the world," she says, showing us a picture of a Communist Chinese representative seated on a Rigden Ranch gelding.

"My brother (John Hays) is a state senator (now on the governor's staff) and he travels to many parts of the world representing Arizona agriculture. He invites many people here to see a typical American family ranch. We have had people from many nations of the world here."

A picture of Cynthia and John Wayne always attracts the visitor's attention. The famous movie actor purchased several of Cynthia's bronzes.

"Regardless of where they are from," Margaret says, "they all recognize John Wayne. They may not know a word of English, but they point to that picture and say, `That John Wayne.'"

"This is one hell'va outfit, ain't it?" Tom jests. "Run by a blind man and two women."

Margaret not only loves to cook but collects cookbooks, and while she owns a stack of them, she hardly ever uses one, and seldom goes by a recipe. "Oh, it's just a little of this and a little of that," she laughs.

"That's real funny," says Tom. "I worked my way through high school by selling Kirkland Women's Club cookbooks. They only cost a dollar and I sold a bunch of 'em, but Margaret won't even use one." Tom tells us about his favorite dish, what he calls the cowboy's staple diet, "Beans, jerky and bull ass gravy." Before they had iceboxes, Tom says, everyone lived on jerky.

"Cut it up and hang it in the barn to dry. Most of the time we'd have it all et up before it cured."

Margaret has the same trouble with much of her cooking; it gets et up almost before it comes to the table.

Margaret Rigden's Pastel de Elote
(Mexican Corn Bread)

½ lb. butter or shortening

1 cup sugar

4 eggs

1 can green chiles

½ cup grated Jack cheese

1 can cream style corn

½ cup grated sharp cheddar cheese

¼ tablespoon salt

1 cup flour

1 cup yellow corn meal

4 teaspoons baking soda

Preheat oven to 350 degrees. Mix all ingredients together in a bowl and pour into an

8" x 12" x 2" pan.

Reduce heat to 300 degrees and bake for one hour.

Serves ten hungry hands, good for hors d'oeuvres or between meal snacks.

Tom, Cynthia and some of the hands will, many times, pack Pastel de Elote in their saddle bags on long rides.

The ranch cook's call to dinner. Photograph by Charles Belden.

SECTION IV:
THE GREAT BASIN

If the cowboy won his national fame on the trails and in the
Kansas cowtowns, the range and ranch frontier provided him
with respectability and made him an admirably romantic
folk type.

Joe M. Frantz and Julian Ernest Choate, Jr.,
The American Cowboy: Myth and Reality
University of Oklahoma Press, 1955

Many Americans think of the two Great Basin states of Nevada and Utah as an enigma; Nevada seems to mean just the gambling world of Las Vegas and Reno and not much more. Many associate Utah with the Great Salt Lake, the Mormon Tabernacle Choir and skiing, as the state's license plate boasts.

But these wonderfully scenic and historic areas feature much more than just the common presumptions about them. For example, the Nevada Commission on Tourism named three of the five regions: Covered Wagon Country, Pony Express Territory and Pioneer Territory. Nevada also ranks seventh in terms of overall geographic size.

Around 1776, Spanish priest Father Francesco Graces entered the state looking for a new route to California. Though he may have been the first European to come to Nevada, not until the 1820s did trappers ply their trade in the area. In 1850 the first permanent settlement, Genoa, grew around a Mormon trading post.

Americans became conscious of Nevada only with the discovery of gold in the West (particularly the Comstock Lode) during the same year, and then later when silver was found. The Comstock Lode became one of the greatest financial assets for the North during the Civil War and helped in achieving statehood for Nevada. Originally part of the Utah Territory, Nevada became a separate territory in 1861, with statehood declared only three years later, primarily because the North needed two more votes to pass the Thirteenth Amendment, abolishing slavery.

The towering mountains, multi-colored canyons and fertile valleys of Utah, so resembling the Holy Land in topography, became the Mormon's chosen settlement site.

But in 1776 Fathers Escalante and Dominguez discovered the area while searching for a direct route from Santa Fe, New Mexico to Monterey, California. In 1824 famed mountain men Jim Bridger and Etienne Provost discovered the Great Salt Lake.

Almost a hundred years after the two fathers had passed through, Brigham Young and his Mormon followers founded Salt Lake City. Many feared the Mormon theocracy, which did not seem in line with the mainstream American thinking of the day, and so not until 1896 did the area become a state.

Today, beef production and dairy cattle alone account for half of Utah's agricultural income, with sheep and horses also making a major economic contribution to the state.

Nevada is also a big ranching and cowboy state. The annual Cowboy Poetry Gathering held each January in Elko marks the importance of cowboys to the state. During the festival, non-cowboys, non-buckaroos and non-ranchers might almost feel as if they were in a foreign country. The granddaddy of such events, the festival celebrates the cowboy way of life as hundreds of participants in their own distinctive dress tell stories and share experiences, music and, of course poetry, which affirms the cowboy and his traditions.

Nevada is one of those places that seems extremely hostile to human life, a desert that is the driest place in the nation. While precious metal may have provided the first attraction to the state, for ranchers, the wide open spaces and the gold camps needing a ready source of beef were the first draw. In the latter part of the 1800s the railroads attracted more ranchers to the Great Basin.

Today cattle and sheep graze on more than 55 million acres of private and public Nevada rangeland. Buckaroos, who see themselves just a bit differently from ordinary cowboys, tend Nevada's cattle. Maybe it's too extreme to say the buckaroo views himself as just a notch better than the average cowpuncher, but working mostly in Nevada, California, Oregon, southern Idaho and parts of Utah, the buckaroo has taken his distinctive dress and his particular traditions from what he calls the real Old West, originating from Spanish customs but now developed into its own particular style.

Originally named for the vaquero, the buckaroo wears an old-time crease in his hat, his neck scarf is silk, he wears chinks (short chaps with leather fringe), holds his pants up with suspenders instead of a belt and carries a pocket watch. He tucks his pants into high boots with big underslung heels and his silver spurs have large rowels. He likes elaborate and expensive gear and he loves silver frills on his saddle or anywhere he can have some decoration. He loves silver..silver..silver.

Maybe these buckaroos don't fully understand what the old days were all about. Not everyone chose to be a cowboy for the romance now associated with the profession.

In 1862, for example, a Kentuckian got a job on a roundup crew in the Great Basin.

He wrote in his journal, "Here I am on my way into the heart of a country known to be inhabited by hostile Indians...And why? Because I have the misfortune to be broke." This cowpoke was hardly making a decision based on a career preference. He acted from necessity, just as many of his cohorts have before and since then.

In fact, cowboys all over the West had a tough life. Their work was dirty, tedious and very, very dangerous.

As one historian wrote, "Far from being a handsome lover, the typical cowboy was apt to have a crooked nose that had been broken at least once, a game leg, a hernia, a finger or two that had never mended satisfactorily after a fracture, and a couple of teeth missing...cowboys worked hard on the range and raised hell when they came to town, which was not very often. They were a group distinct from their employers, who were always called ranchers or ranchmen."

Perhaps these words might be a bit exaggerated, but the range cowboys were hardly the dandies Hollywood has presented—cowboys who never got dirty and had plenty of time to be in town, away from the ranch and ranch business.

Large numbers of sheep outfits also created a unique development in the Basin, particularly in Nevada, influenced by the influx of the Basque. Proud sheepherding people from the Pyrenees Mountains, located on the border between France and Spain, the Basques maintain their own language, which they say goes back to the beginning of all tongues. They bring with them their own distinct traditions that are neither French nor Spanish. After arriving in California, they made their way inland where they became sheepherders, just as in their native lands. The Basques eventually became flock owners. Many have clung to their own traditions.

A herder often took part of his pay each year in ewes (female sheep), herding his sheep with those of his employer. When the herder amassed a large enough flock, he went out on his own, grazing his sheep wherever he could—often on public land, so available in the Great Basin.

With their own language, their own customs and even their own diet, the Basques have added a rich cultural layer to this region that still endures. Basque festivals are held in many areas here throughout the year.

Today both Nevada and Utah remain part of the vast open spaces of the West. Except for population centers like Las Vegas, Reno and Salt Lake, this magnificent desert and mountain landscape, complete with its ranches, is still sparsely populated and appears much as it did a hundred years ago when that busted cowboy took a roundup job to keep body and soul together.

SEARLE RANCHES
VERNAL, UTAH

SHREWD TRADING AND TENDER KIDS
Vonetta Searle, Old-Time Cook

We pulled into Vernal, Utah (population 7,300) one spring morning in late May, immediately impressed with the cleanliness and beautiful setting of the town. Located in Utah's northeast corner below Wyoming where Highway 40 meets 191, Vernal is in the flat country west of Desolation Canyon, a deep chasm rivaling the Grand Canyon and cut by the Green River as it flows south from Flaming Gorge Reservoir.

We knew no one in Vernal, so we stopped at the Uintah County extension office to get acquainted with the area and see if we could meet some local ranchers, cowboys and cooks.

The name Searle kept coming up in conversation. "Vonetta Searle is probably the best ranch cook in these parts," the locals told us. We made a phone call and Vonetta invited us out. Woody and Vonetta Searle live in a spacious, modern ranch house at the top of a hill on the south side of town, overlooking Ashley Valley. Though a short visit, because Vonetta was busy and Woody was ill, we thoroughly enjoyed our trip. Vonetta is an excellent cook, and Woody also loves to tinker in the kitchen.

Most ranches have trouble keeping one cook in the kitchen, but at the Searle outfit, Vonetta and Woody argue about who's the best cook and who can prepare the tastiest meals.

"Woody's the best cook," Vonetta defers. "No doubt about it. He cooks lamb ribs in a Dutch oven, and let me tell you, it is good."

"I do cook some good ribs," Woody says. "The secret is to cook the lamb in its own tallow. My lamb ribs get better each time they are heated and re-served. I will admit they're delicious, and I've never met a person who didn't like 'em and ask for more."

The Searles, both in their early seventies, are semi-retired, and let their grown children look after most of the ranching business.

"We have a big blow-out up here each year on our wedding anniversary," Vonetta says. "We invite over 300 people up and Woody fills 'em up on ribs."

Woody grins and says, "Vonetta's the cook. I just work here."

Both the Searles have worked in the Vernal area all their lives. Born near Vernal, Vonetta grew up on a ranch. Her father ran sheep and later worked as a government trapper. Vonetta and Woody chatted about the area's history.

A BACKWARD GLANCE

As in many places in the West, early trappers and mountain men first came to Ashley Valley to make a living. The first known white men passed through the Vernal area in the late 1770s. The journals of Fray Francisco Anastasio Dominguez and Fray Sivestre Velez De Escalante relate how, on September 13, 1776, they camped on the Green River above present-day Jensen, just east of Vernal, almost 30 years before Lewis and Clark came west in search of the fabled Northwest Passage.

The Ashley Valley area has long been occupied by Indians. Prehistoric tribal petroglyphs can still be found in the valley. One of the earliest tribal peoples, known as the basketmakers, mysteriously disappeared, but when white men first came to the area the Ute Indians were living there. The state's name, Utah, comes from these "Uintah-ats" Indians.

The town of Vernal formed when nervous settlers "forted up" after the massacre of some whites in nearby Meeker, Colorado in 1879. The residents wanted to call their new town Ashley Center in honor of William Ashley, an early trapper and mountain man for whom the valley was named. But an Ashley town already existed, so the name of Vernal was adopted to appease the postmaster.

"We were born just before the Great Depression," Vonetta said. "We were very poor, and never knew anything but hard work." While still a teenager, Woody saw his father killed by lightning as he drove cattle. Soon afterwards, Woody took over running the outfit and he's been a rancher ever since.

"Although there were times during the Depression I had to do a little trapping myself to keep the ranch afloat," he says.

Besides being a cowboy, a trapper and a sheepman, Woody was a shrewd trader. He bought, sold and traded hides; and he also traded livestock. Vonetta says that Woody always had two or three projects going at the same time.

Today, the Searles own two ranches, as well as a large restaurant in Vernal and their suburban home.

They keep trying to retire, but business ventures crop up and Woody keeps wheeling and dealing.

"We're just common, everyday folk," Vonetta says. "We're not fancy. We like simple pleasures, like dancing at the senior citizens center on Friday nights and Woody's liver, onion and fry bread breakfasts."

Woody says what he really enjoys is visiting with the kids and grandkids and traveling to see different country; but his favorite pleasure remains Vonetta's cooking.

And so as the Searles kept complimenting one another on their kitchen skills, arguing that the other was far and away the superior ranch cook, we wondered half in jest whether their ongoing good-natured dispute might just be a clever ruse to stay out of the kitchen. We wanted to get a recipe from Woody, but Mr. Searle insisted that Vonetta is the cook; we decided not to argue with Woody. He might have traded us out of our van, and we'd have been afoot in Indian country.

Vonetta's Chocolate Delight Cake

> 2 cups flour
> 4 tablespoons cocoa
> 1 tablespoon baking soda
> 2 cups sugar
> 1 cup water
> 2 sticks (½ pound) margarine, melted
> ¼ cup buttermilk
> 2 eggs
> 1 tablespoon vanilla

Sift together the flour, cocoa, baking soda and sugar. Bring the water, margarine, and buttermilk to a boil and add the dry ingredients. Stir in the eggs and vanilla.

Grease and flour a large sheet pan. Bake at 400 degrees F. for 20-25 minutes. While the cake is baking:

> 1 stick (¼ pound) margarine
> 4 tablespoons cocoa
> 6 tablespoons buttermilk
> 3 cups powdered sugar
> 1 tablespoon vanilla
> 1 cup chopped nuts

Bring the margarine, cocoa and buttermilk to a boil. Add the remainder of the ingredients. Set aside, let cool a few minutes, then add spread.

Frost the cake and serve.

Yield: 1 cake

DUVAL RANCH
WELLS, NEVADA

FROM FARM HAND TO BUCKAROO
Grace Duval, Quick Ranch Cook

A cowboy we knew who worked at the Duval Ranch gave us directions to the place. A native of Spokane, Washington, Bernard Harris calls himself a Mutant Son of the Sage. Everyone else just called him Harris. We first met him on his first job at the McDowell Ranch in Montana. Harris went down a long, hard road to become a cowboy; he started out as a farm hand and worked his way up to buckaroo on some of the biggest outfits in the West.

Harris was still apprenticing as one of two hired hands at the the Duval Ranch, a family operation. We arrived during late winter to find Harris laid up with a bum leg, the result of a horse wreck. He lived alone in the modern bunkhouse which was attached to the vehicle shop. He spent his time hobbling around doing chores, trying to hold down his job. All he could talk about was getting away from the Duvals and hiring on with one of the big loop outfits that make Nevada so popular with buckaroos. Harris was probably better off at the Duval than anywhere he could have been. The Duvals treated him like family and were kind and gentle teachers.

The Duval Ranch runs only Hereford cattle.

About 36 miles south and west of Wells in the Ruby Valley, the Duval Ranch is situated between the Ruby Mountains and the Cherry Creek Mountains. Don Duval was born in this 6,500-foot-high valley. We noticed that the valley resembles the Big Hole Valley in Montana. The area gets a lot of moisture from snowmelt in the surrounding mountains, and the valley floor is pocked with marshes and bog holes. Grass grows well here because of the shallow water table and the sub-irrigated pastures.

Given to Don's grandmother as a wedding present, the ranch house still provides a home for Don's mother. The cow barn, corrals, and the horse barn are situated a short distance to the south of the bunkhouse Don and his wife Grace live just up the road at the old Gulager place that belonged to Don's aunt, also given to her as a wedding present. Don's great-grandparents were French Canadians and homesteaded in the Ruby Valley and in nearby Clover Valley.

Don says that his mother lived on the old Overland Ranch as a young girl and her father served as a soldier at the Fort Ruby, which kept the peace during the Indian Wars. When this soldier-father died, he left a widow and seven children to fend for themselves on the frontier. A strong pioneer woman, Don's grandmother raised the youngsters by herself on a ranch, now part of the Ruby Valley National Wildlife Refuge.

Grace hails from Delta, Colorado where she lived on a small farm near town. She says that her mother rode a mule and delivered mail in the county where they lived. The Duvals get mail deliveries only three times a week now, but Grace says she likes living in the country.

The Duval Ranch runs only Hereford cattle. Don says, "I kinda like to have 'em all alike. We hold our calves over, feed 'em through the winter, and sell 'em as yearlings. Maybe we lose a little efficiency and hybrid thriftiness, but we haven't had any trouble finding buyers. The buyers still like Herefords. We do have trouble with sunburned and windchapped bags on cows, and do have to do a lot of doctoring on that in the spring, especially if there is lots of snow coupled with lots of sun."

A HARROWING NIGHT

Grace says they used to breed yearling heifers, so that they would calve as two-year-olds, but found that they had fewer problems if they didn't breed young cows until they were in their second year.

"You have to feed 'em one more year, but it's so much easier on the cows, and it's a hell'va lot easier on us," Grace says. "One time we had to do two C-sections in one night. I had a ewe ready to lamb, and at the same time, the heifer got into trouble and we cut the calf out. No sooner did we get it on its feet when another heifer was panicking and we cut that calf out. When we got that done we were just sagging against the wall, exhausted, trying to catch our breath. I looked over at my ewe and she had lambed, and the poor little things were dead. I had been so busy with the calves that I had forgotten all about the lambs.

"It was a bloody mess. We were covered with blood. At the time I still had small children at home, and when Don and I came back in the house, it was about 4 o'clock in the morning. The kids were up and they said, `Mother, what in the world happened to you and Dad—did you have a fight?'" Don has taken courses in ranch veterinary medicine at the community college in Elko and has attended clinics on emergency vet procedures.

"I think there must be a rule of nature that says you never get to do a Caesarian in the daytime. We've had to do all ours at night. Always late at night and always in poor light," Don says.

SOME BAD BREAKS AND SOME COYOTE TROUBLE

Don rode bareback and saddle bronc in amateur rodeos when he was younger and was never injured, but has broken both legs in horse falls while doing ranch work. In 1960 he broke one leg in seven places when a horse fell on him.

"I was chasing a calf that escaped from the bunch, and my pony hit a patch of ice and down we went. Having a horse fall on you is the worst thing that can happen to a cowboy."

During summers, the Duvals put on extra hands to help with irrigating and haying, and Grace cooks for all the crew, year-round. She also raises sheep, chickens, ducks and geese and grows a large garden. She says coyotes give her lots of trouble when the predators steal her fowl and kill her sheep.

She also has problems with skunks and raccoons in the chicken house.

"One year the raccoons completely wiped me out of the chicken business. They killed every one we had," she says.

Grace works hard to keep her garden growing, but Don says, "Raising a garden in this valley is more good luck than good management. We get our last frost about June 26 and our first frost about August 26—a damn short growing season."

Grace agrees, but still plants a garden every year and says she likes lots of fresh vegetables on her table.

She likes to prepare a zucchini casserole she says has proven a favorite with the ranch hands.

"We had one boy here and he told me he didn't like zucchini. But when I served this casserole, he ate the whole damn thing and asked for more."

Grace Duval's Quick Cowboy Zucchini Casserole

3 to 4 zucchini, diced
1 onion, chopped
4 teaspoons butter
1 cup grated carrots
2 stalks celery, diced
1 cup dry, seasoned bread crumbs
1 10½-ounce can cream of mushroom or celery soup
½ cup sour cream
1 cup grated cheddar cheese

Cover the zucchini with water and bring to a boil. Remove, drain, and place in a casserole pan.

Saute the onion in the butter. Add the carrots, celery, bread crumbs, soup, and sour cream, and mix.

Pour the mixture over the zucchini and top with the grated cheese.

Bake at 375 degrees F. for 30 minutes or until cooked through.

Serves: 4 to 6

PARIS SHEEP & CATTLE COMPANY
ELY, NEVADA

HOME OF WILD HORSES
Mary Jean Paris, Basque Ranch Cook

The White Pine County Extension Agent in Ely, over in the east-central part of the state, told us we just had to visit Mary Jean and Pete Paris, so we tooled up Highway 93 to about 20 miles north of town and turned west at Cherry Creek, crossed the Egan Mountains and drove another 28 miles up a dirt road in Butte Valley before we found the Paris Ranch. We passed only a couple of other ranches during our entire drive. This is wide open country here.

The road over the pass was once used by Pony Express riders as they beat feet between Reno and Salt Lake City. Goshute Indians, hunters and gatherers whose diet included bugs, grasshoppers and anything they could catch, once inhabited the surrounding country.

In the late 1800s, Basque sheepherders moved their flocks into the 6,500-foot- high valley, home to deer, antelope and wild horses—lots of wild horses.

As we picked our way to the Paris place, a stallion, six mares and two colts galloped alongside the van for a quarter of a mile before crossing the road and disappearing over a ridge, manes flowing in the wind, and tails held up, a sign of independence and freedom.

BASQUE SHEEPMAN OF THE WEST

Just off the road, the Paris Ranch headquarters consists of a modern, single-level ranch house, a large vehicle shop, a white, wood-frame barn and pole corrals. A few elm and cottonwood trees provide shade in summer and a windbreak in winter. Pete's father, Beltran Paris, a Basque sheepman, came to Nevada from the Pyrenees Mountains near the French and Spanish border. Beltran saved his meager sheepherder wages, and in 1918 started his own ranch with 1,900 sheep, one burro and two dogs.

In 1926 he acquired the current Paris Ranch and today the Paris Sheep and Cattle Company extends across three Nevada counties.

William A. Douglas, professor of anthropology, University of Nevada, Reno, wrote *Beltran, Basque Sheepman of the American West*, a book about the life and hard times of this Nevada pioneer. Beltran survived fights over water and grass, and struggles with rustlers, coyotes, cougars and government officials. The Basque sheepman passed on a legacy of thriftiness and toughness to his sons.

In his book, Douglas writes, "Beltran Paris lived a life of unceasingly hard work and few expectations."

Today on the Paris Ranch there is still lots of hard work to do, but living conditions have gradually improved.

Pete says, "We got gas lamps when I was a kid and that was a hell'va big improvement. In about 1940 we got a diesel-generated electricity plant and that sure was nice. In 1975 we got rural electricity and that was another big improvement."

Up until 1980, the Paris Ranch communicated with the outside world by two-way radio. Today they have a radio-telephone, but still get mail delivered only twice a week, and one of the boys has to drive 25 miles to Cherry Creek to pick it up.

A UNITED NATIONS CAFETERIA

Raised on a French farm, Mary Jean says the isolation in Butte Valley doesn't bother her a bit. "I love it here. I cook and I bake and I help out with the ranch work where I can. I'm happy being here with Pete and the boys."

Pete and Mary Jean's three sons are grown, and continue the Paris tradition of raising sheep and cattle. One son operates the cattle business the other the sheep business and the third is a CPA in Elko and keeps track of all the ranch's business. A fourth son was killed in a tragic car accident. The 'boys' to whom Mary Jean refers are young Spanish herders and cowboys who intern on the ranch as part of an agricultural exchange program. Mary Jean and Pete both speak French, Spanish and Basque as well as English, and mealtimes at the ranch sound like table talk at a United Nations cafeteria.

For sixteen years, while her sons were growing up, Mary Jean and her sons stayed in Ely, so the boys could attend school. She came out to the ranch on weekends and holidays and did all her housecleaning and cooking for the whole week. "That was the hardest thing I've ever had to do," she says.

Well, almost the hardest...Mary Jean graduated from high school at age twelve and worked for the next three years as a nanny.

Then World War II came and the good times ended. During the war Mary Jean supported herself by cooking, and was chef in a hotel restaurant when the Germans took over France in 1939.

"For us, the war only lasted a year," she says. "But the occupation of France lasted five years. The Germans took everything." Mary Jean says that they were allowed to have potatoes only once a week and meat once a week, and a very small portion at that.

She says she never saw an egg from 1939 until France was liberated by the Allies in 1944.

"Believe me," she said, "I learned to cook the conservative way. Even today I don't waste a thing. When I prepare a meal and set it out, I keep setting it out until it is all gone."

Mary Jean may still cook the conservative way, but now she doesn't have to cook quite as much or as often as she did in earlier years.

"When we were lambing and had a large crew of herders, we'd butcher a mutton a week for ourselves and one for the men." Now Pete's brother Bert runs the lambing camp and his wife Wendy does the cooking.

Sometimes Mary Jean and Pete and the boys will help Bert and Wendy trail sheep over the mountains and across the desert to their summer range near Las Vegas, a trip of over 300 miles. In fall, the sheep trail back and winter on the open ridges south of Elko.

Pete admits that sheep require more care than cattle. "Coyotes are a constant problem—year-round. We have a government trapper that is supposed to help us, but he ain't much good. He lives in Ely and we call him if we have a problem, but by the time he gets here, them dogs are long gone."

Mountain lions also cause plenty of problems with his sheep. "I've seen the time an old cat would come in here and kill 20 to 60 lambs in one night. A rancher can't stand that kind of loss," Pete says.

Wild horses cause another of Pete's headaches. He has about 200 head on his range at all times. "The BLM is supposed to keep 'em thinned out, but I don't think much of the

BLM and their efforts. They try—but they never seem to get the job done." Horses, wild or broken, have been a constant problem for Pete. He says a sheepherder's horse is supposed to be the oldest, gentlest horse on the ranch, but a sheepherding horse bucked him off and broke his shoulder not too long ago. He says he'll always remember that accident, because he's reminded of the injury every time the weather changes.

Now fully recovered from that wreck, Pete still gets around the ranch and checks stock a-horseback. He tried raising horses for sale but that didn't prove out.

"We'd get about fifty percent fillies every year, and you couldn't hardly sell 'em," Pete says. He sticks to commercial cattle and crosses Red Angus bulls on Hereford heifers.

"We used to use longhorn bulls, but by God, I couldn't sell the calves. I was taking a 10-cent loss on every pound. I can't afford that."

The Parises have also had their problems with poultry. "We tried chickens, but it gets so damn cold up here that half of 'em froze to death in the winter. We tried geese, but they are the messiest things on God's green earth. We finally decided that we've worked all our lives to make this a cattle ranch and we'd better stick with what we know best."

Mary Jean knows cooking best. She whomped up a batch of French steaks for us that we'll never forget. Wonderful hosts, the Paris family are real Westerners who like to visit and are never too busy to talk to someone from the outside. We thoroughly enjoyed our visit.

Mary Jean's French Steaks

4 1-inch thick or better round or shoulder steaks
(Great using mutton, too.)
Flour seasoned with salt and garlic powder
4 tablespoons vegetable oil
1 onion, sliced
1 bell pepper, stem and seeds removed, sliced
1 large can tomato sauce
¼ cup catsup

Roll the steaks in flour, covering all sides. Sear the steaks on both sides in a hot skillet with 2 tablespoons vegetable oil. Remove the steaks from the skillet.

Saute the onion and pepper in the remaining oil until soft.

Combine the tomato sauce and catsup.

Place steaks in baking pan and cover with the onion and pepper. Pour sauce over top. Cover with foil and bake at 325 degrees F. for one hour.

Serves: 4

Variation: Substitute mushroom sauce for the tomato and cook at 300 degrees F. for one hour.

WINE CUP RANCH
WELLS, NEVADA

HOT SPRINGS AND WHOREHOUSES
Doug Ferris, Ornery Ranch Cook

We pulled into the Wine Cup Ranch just because we liked the sign over their entrance gate. Located about eighteen miles north of Wells, the Wine Cup headquarters is barely visible from Highway 93. Elaine Black, wife of Manager Martin Black, greeted us as we drove up.

We learned that Elaine is a daughter of Ray Hunt, internationally known horse trainer and author of *Think Harmony with Horses*, one of the best books written on horse training.

We explained to Elaine our mission of visiting ranches throughout the West and interviewing cooks, and she invited us to stay at the ranch a couple of days. She told us that the Wine Cup had one of the best cooks in the West. At first we thought Elaine, being the Western woman she is, may have been telling us a windy, a tall tale, but after two days of visiting with her, Martin, and Doug Ferris, the cook, we were convinced. If he wasn't the best, he surely was among the top two or three ranch cooks. Ferris certainly proved one of the most interesting cooks we had spoken to in a long time.

Martin never said how many acres the Wine Cup encompassed or how many cattle they ran, but the ranch is one of several owned by the Nevada-Pacific Power Company. Jimmy Stewart, renowned movie star, previously owned the Wine Cup. Built like a motel, the old headquarters has three wings constructed in a triangle, housing apartments facing a swimming pool in the center of a court. Geothermal water piped from a series of hot springs heats the buildings and pools.

Martin says he doesn't know who owned the ranch before Stewart, but Doug said gangsters from Reno owned the place and operated it as a brothel, which accounted for the layout of the buildings, so the boss could see everybody at all times. "It used to be just a big old whorehouse. Looks like a whorehouse, don't it?"

We declined to comment on that remark, but Doug proved something of an expert, so we took his word.

While we visited, the old whorehouses were being torn down, as the ranch was getting down to the more serious business of raising horses and cattle. Martin is a serious young cowman who makes his own bridles and ropes out of braided horsehair and flies a company airplane to check on cattle and cowboys in the ranch's far-reaching pastures.

"We still do a lot of work a-horseback," Martin says. "We raise and train all our own horses. A good horse is still a very important part of this operation. Without horses we'd never get our work done around here." All the Wine Cup horses are trained using the Ray Hunt method, and the old master occasionally stops by to visit Elaine and put on a clinic for Martin and the cowboys.

A Fancy Hotel Chef

Martin and the cowboys were busy while we were there and we didn't want to get in the way, so we stayed in a little two-man bunkhouse that Elaine used as a schoolhouse for her two boys because they hadn't started regular school yet. We spent all day with Doug Ferris, and he filled our ears as well as our bellies.

Born near St. George, Utah in 1920, Doug was raised in a mining camp nearby, where his mother was a cook. He said he has spent his entire life in kitchens. After he left home, he found work in several kitchens in nearby Las Vegas.

"Worked for them gangsters in their fancy hotels," he says with a wink. Elaine says Doug has been chef in some of the best restaurants in the West and has worked in Vegas, Reno, and San Francisco. Doug has even owned several restaurants.

His wife died of cancer in 1984, and Doug says, "The fuzz just sort of went off the peach for me when she passed on. She was the only person I ever loved." He says he now cooks on ranches because they take care of him, and he adds, "Once you start cooking on a ranch you can't stop. Especially me. I'm a drinking man and a gambler, and sooner or later I'll get down and out; and I always return to cooking. The ranch gives me a nice place to work and sleep and they make sure I've got everything I need. I can't ask for more than that."

In his early years of traveling around the country, Doug even tried his hand at working on a sheep ranch in Montana back in 1938.

"That tying wool is the hardest job I ever had in my whole life. All them ticks all over your body and that grease on your feet and legs; I didn't like that one bit."

He says working in a bakery proved to be the second-hardest job he's ever held. "In a bakery you never get to move around. Just stand in one place and roll out dough 10 hours without a break. I didn't like that either."

Doug starting holding down cooking jobs in 1939. Cooks, like cowboys, move around a lot and like to see a lot of different country. Doug says he has seen his share of kitchens and country.

Dean Tobis, manager of the Gamble Ranch, sister ranch of the Wine Cup, verified that cooks come and go, and said that good cooks are hard to find and harder to hold after you hire them. He's hired drunken cooks in town and driven them 40 miles out to the ranch.

"Lots of times them old boys would never cook a meal. As soon as they sobered up and saw where they were, they'd quit right on the spot."

Ornery Ranch Cook Doug Ferris at the Wine Cup Ranch.

A Scowl, a Growl and Buzzard Puke Bob

Doug came to the Wine Cup in 1986. "Elaine and I raise the leppies (orphaned calves) and hogs and we got a hundred chickens. We sell the eggs and they let me keep the egg money (Doug also takes care of the chickens). Last month I made $30. Now that's a damn nice bonus." Unlike most ranches, the Wine Cup keeps beer in the kitchen cooler. "They ain't too happy about it, but they know it makes me happy, so no one says much about it."

Keeping a cook happy is almost an impossible task, because most cooks seem grouchy by nature and stay in a bad mood all the time, probably because they would rather be doing something else—drinking and gambling, maybe. Cowboys say cooks are very even-tempered—mad all the time. They give cooks a wide berth. Even good-natured Doug can be grouchy. Cowboys at the Wine Cup may enter the dining hall before meals, but they can't eat until Doug sets the food on the table. He sets the table with a scowl and a growl. "I'm your grouchy cook, not your friendly waitress. There it is; eat it or wear it," Doug mutters. Most of the time leaving the cook alone proves the best policy for cowboys. But the hands at the Wine Cup told us they once had a cook that was so mean that even ignoring him didn't work. They called him Buzzard Puke Bob.

"He was so bad it was unreal. He never took a bath and he stank like a skunk. His cooking was so bad we started eating sardines and crackers in the bunkhouse and staying out of the kitchen, but that just made him mad. One day he fixed up what he thought was a nice dinner and no one showed up, so he took his old pickup and drove it right through the bunkhouse. Luckily no one got hurt."

The boys at the Wine Cup don't have to worry about Doug driving anywhere. He lost his license on his last little spree in Elko.

"I'd had a little too much to drink and I sideswiped 19 parked cars before I got 'er stopped. They said they was lifting my license to do the county a favor." Nowadays when Doug has a day off, he catches a ride into town with Martin or Elaine or someone from the ranch going into Elko to shop.

Doug doesn't do any shopping himself, but he plans his meals well in advance and uses lots of methods to recycle leftovers. He orders supplies once a month and says that works out. "I try not to worry the boss. Hell, he's busy running a ranch. He ain't got time to be bothered by the cook." This same kind of advice Doug dishes out to the young cowboys who come and go on the ranch.

"A lot of these boys won't like the way things are going here and will quit and go into town and complain to the bartender. I tell 'em, 'If you've got a problem, talk it over with the boss and he'll help get it straightened out. Hell, don't tell the bartender. He don't give a shit.'"

Doug's short with young cowboys on the ranch and demands promptness at meal-times. Some ranches fire hands for being late at mealtimes and slowing the cook's schedule. Many, like the Wine Cup, will buy the tardy cowboy a watch and deduct it from his wages.

"I always tell the boss when I go to a new outfit that I want the wine and watch concession," Doug says.

Effortless as a Cat

Doug spoils the hands at the Wine Cup by keeping cookies or pastries out for them at all times and the coffee pot always on. "Hell, some of these boys drink so much coffee, you'd think there was bourbon in it," says Doug. It is a rare ranch where the hands can visit the cookhouse any time they are around. Doug's coffee is exceptionally good and he says that he has tried to show people how to make good coffee, "But people in town, you know, are pretty helpless. That's why I'd rather cook out in the country." The Wine Cup doesn't send out a wagon on roundups any more, and Doug said that he misses that. "In the cooking business, it's the housekeeping that breaks your back. On a wagon you don't have a house, and life is a hell'va lot easier out there." Washing dishes bothers him not the least bit and is one of the things he does best. "Some really big outfits have a dishwasher. One time I got caught with my finger in the dishwasher and we both got fired."

At the Wine Cup, the crew is probably not aware of what they are eating most of the time. Doug's large and long restaurant experience gives him a wide range of dishes to prepare, but he sighs and admits that his only reward is seeing food packed away by hungry hands.

"Most of these boys ain't never et in no fancy restaurant like where I worked. Hell, half the stuff I fix 'em, they don't even know what it is."

Doug bakes a lot and keeps about twenty loaves of bread made up and frozen at all times. When the crews work away from headquarters, Doug prepares sandwiches, as well as drinks and fruit. "I make sure they get their veggies and not so much starch and junk."

Doug cooks on an old gas-fired South Bend range, and he moves about the kitchen as effortlessly as a cat. His motions are fluid and smooth with no wasted movement in anything he does. He never measures anything, and he never looks at a clock. Yet all his dishes come out perfectly prepared and precisely on time. A cowboy, sitting on a bench sipping coffee, glances at his watch, probably one that was forced on him. Doug scowls. "What the hell you looking at your watch for? Ain't nobody here taking any medicine. Ain't no damn bus coming. Don't worry about the time. Time will take care of itself."

Times, however, are a-changing, and Doug thinks that a lot of fun has gone out of ranching, with big corporations buying up many of the family-owned outfits. "It seems that there is more tension now-days. Bosses are serious. Hell, we used to have fun on a ranch. Now they don't even want you to take a drink or have a woman come out. How they expect a man to enjoy himself?"

HORSE ORDERS

Doug thinks ranches need more old-fashioned cooks who have been down the road and learned the ropes of cowboy cooking. But he says that those old-timers are fast fading from the ranching scene. "I was gonna sew up a roast, so I asked the boss to get me a larding needle in town and the guy there told him, `Hell, cooks who use them things are all dead.' We had to take a big old harness needle and open the eye, and I used that. Most cooks now-days just cook a roast in a sack. Shit, anyone can do that." Doug also scorns cooks who fabricate tales about sourdough starter. "To make sourdough, I just make my starter a day or two ahead. I don't keep a starter. Hell, that's too much trouble. I tell the boys it's a hundred years old; that's what all these cooks tell you. It's all just a big joke."

Doug doesn't joke around in his kitchen, and he's serious and sober when it comes to cooking. In his restaurants he was known as a blanch man, one who specializes in soups and sauces. He has some advice for cooks who are serious about their cooking. "Once you open catsup, leave it sit at room temperature. If you put it in the refrigerator and take it out, it'll sour. Every Monday I make barbecue sauce and use up all the old catsup."

Another of Doug's specialties is his deep-fried cauliflower. "Take a couple of good-sized cauliflower heads and chop 'em up into one-inch-sized pieces. Cook 'em at a low boil for one hour. Drain, mix a batter of eggs and flour and dip the pieces in. Heat cooking oil and fry the pieces until they are crisp.

"Makes a good side dish or horse orders (hors d'oeuvres). I've had people ask me, `What kind of fish is that?' I tell 'em, `Sea bass,' and they believe me. It's quick and easy and really tastes good. When all the big corporate execs come up for our annual Christmas party, I fix up a batch of `Sea Bass' and they hog it right down."

Though Doug is Italian and prepares lots of dishes from the old country, he also serves lots of Southwest staples like beans or refried beans.

"To make good refries, you gotta cook 'em in an iron skillet. First cook 'em your regular way, then grease your skillet, put your beans in and top 'em with chopped onions. Sprinkle with paprika and cover with grated cheese. It makes a real good meal."

Elaine said that Doug is a real old-time ranch cook and they feel very fortunate to have him at the Wine Cup. "He's a real treasure. He spoils us, that's for sure. I hope we can keep him here forever.

"But while Doug is very content at the Wine Cup, he is ever the old cowboy cook and is not sure how long he'll stay anywhere. "I like cooking and I'm thinking about writing a book about it. I'm gonna call it Fifty Years In America's Kitchens. I'll buy me a big old motor home and hire me a purty woman to drive it and I'll go down the road one more time."

Doug Ferris' Ornery Ranch Cook Barbecue Sauce

Following to taste:

2 medium onions, chopped

4 cloves garlic, chopped

1 cup water

1 tablespoon chili powder

24 oz. bottle catsup

2 4-oz. cans tomato sauce

1 teaspoon oregano leaves

1 6-oz. can tomato paste

2 bay leaves

4 cubes chicken broth

¼ teaspoon garlic powder

½ cup brown sugar

1 teaspoon paprika

1 teaspoon Worcestershire sauce

1 teaspoon Tabasco sauce

Sauté the onions and garlic in an iron skillet. Add the remaining ingredients and simmer for one hour. Add water for desired consistency.

INDEX

SAUCES
  Doug Ferris' Ornery Ranch Cook Barbecue Sauce 142
Sheila's Sloppy Joe Bubble Burgers 54

VENISON
  Tyson Ranch Chili 16
Vera Spring's Chicken Supreme 65
Vonetta's Chocolate Delight Cake 131

ZUCCHINI
  Grace Duval's Quick Cowboy Zucchini Casserole 134